LEFT OF

LEFT OF THE MAINSTREAM

From DIY Film-maker To Public Service Broadcaster

DOUGLAS ANDERSON

'Douglas is a tall and rather narrow man. It's this perspective that helps him to see over things. It also helps him to back into sharp corners. A unique perspective. Surely worthy of a book or two. Rather handily, this is his book.'
Stuart Murdoch, Belle and Sebastian

'He's one of the very few Scottish people that I actually like.'
Frankie Boyle

'Some people are Scottish. Some people are gentlemen. Some people are cool, generous or funny. Douglas Anderson is somehow all of these things.'
Miles Jupp

CONTENTS

ABOUT THE AUTHOR

As a broadcaster, writer and film-maker, Douglas Anderson has worked extensively for the BBC, Channel 4 and BAFTA specialising in the genres of music and film but also including sport and entertainment. His filmic work has been screened at the BFI and internationally. From Edinburgh, Douglas currently lives in London. This is his second book.

INTRODUCTIONS AND COGITATIONS

The great writer, Cleveland's man of the people, Harvey Pekar once said, "Life is about women, gigs and being creative." I can't disagree, but would also add that injecting some humour wherever possible, whilst also discussing the important minutiae of music and film, is something of an imperative too – and there are certainly elements of that pervading this book.

This is also a tale which deals with the ups and downs of real life, and the good and bad luck that is always prevalent. Although, when it comes to the bad, I like the attitude of German writer Frank Wedekind, who stated, "Any fool can have bad luck; the art exists in knowing how to exploit it."

In any case, if this book were to be viewed as a combination of memoir and at times almost something of a DIY guide, all the while being augmented by some fine ink illustrations, I would see that as a satisfying summation – in fact, it might constitute a pleasing 'three for one offer' of sorts.

I can say with some certainty that you will find out how independent creative projects, such as making no-budget short films with friends, can lead to lucrative broadcasting opportunities. In my case this has involved meeting and interviewing some of the biggest film stars and musicians in the world, and working with greatly admired figures who at one time seemed beyond reach.

However, an early note of caution – if you are after a story that deals with fame and money, and has an ending that ties everything up nicely, then, quite simply, you've got the wrong book. David Niven's *Bring on the Empty Horses* might be a better bet – it's a good read, for sure.

Having said that, there are a multitude of musicians, film stars, broadcasters and directors featured in this book. I've appeared with them all in some capacity, from DIY film-making to professional broadcasting.

There is also a slight outsider status permeating the book at times, and it's certainly the case that I've always felt a bit set apart from the majority. This is in no small part due to my tastes, passions and creative output being located somewhere left of the mainstream.

However, over the years, it didn't deter me from mixing in more mainstream circles, albeit professionally rather than socially. So much so that, at various times, I found myself on national television and radio, working with established mainstream stars – and things became increasingly surreal when the Hollywood A-listers appeared on the scene.

One thing I am sure of is that I am the only person ever to share the screen with the triumvirate of James Mason, Clare Balding and Belle and Sebastian, although, admittedly, not simultaneously.

Regardless, at the same time as appearing on television and radio, I was also undertaking all manner of creative independent projects that were never intended to reach the same size of audience.

I've shared stories of these throughout this book because I strongly believe that maintaining your own creative output is important and beneficial. At the very least, it can be something you have full artistic control over and may even help in securing new exciting opportunities. It can also help in surviving the highs and lows, not just of self-employment, but life in general.

It could even be claimed that this is a story that constitutes something of a journey. A lot of books are about a journey, of course, even if some are contrived just to make a book. Nothing wrong with that per se but it depends on the kind of voyage a particular person wants to undertake. I have little desire to carry a vacuum cleaner around a Baltic state or visit as many restaurants as I can with the word 'food' in the title. The former sounds exhausting and the latter could very likely lead to acid indigestion.

Thankfully, such excursions or gimmicks aren't necessary, as I've already been on a journey – one involving music, writing, film, celebrity, and much else besides. The fact that I nearly died along the way was admittedly an annoyance, but just serves to show there are potential pitfalls in every walk of life.

LONDON, ENGLAND

When people decide to move to London, they normally do so having landed a job, a place at a further education institute or, at the very least, having secured accommodation. I had none of these luxuries when I made the move but it didn't really bother me.

All I wanted was to further my career, and I needed to be in London to do it, plain and simple. Fortunately, at the time I was single and had no kids or mortgage and so no reasons not to take the risk.

A risk is exactly what it was though, with no guarantees that the move would pay off in any way. However, it is always worth bearing in mind that where people's comfort zones are and where the magic happens are usually poles apart.

Here's how that fateful journey unfolded, back in the Spring of 2002.

London or Bus-t

I had made my decision and was determined to stick by it – to leave everything and everyone I knew and move south. I then bought a bus ticket from Edinburgh to London Victoria that was due to leave two weeks later. This, I calculated, would give me enough time to tie up any loose ends and prepare for a big life change. Thankfully, I had little holding me back – but no job prospects at the other end.

Why the bus and not the comparatively much faster and more comfortable train though? It is something I have asked myself a few times since. Well, my choice of budget travel was determined by the fact that I would have to watch my money wisely on arrival in London because of the increased cost of living. On reflection, this was a bad decision and would be proven so in time.

Since buying the ticket, I had heard nothing but horror stories about the bus. These terrifying tales all centred around a variety of complete and utter nut-jobs running amok – from defecating in the aisles to picking fights with anyone who made eye contact with them. The journey undertaken by the protagonists in *Trainspotting* from Edinburgh to London to seal their drug deal seemed a breeze in comparison.

The potential for an unwelcome encounter with a nut-job was most definitely on my mind when, on my night of departure, I attempted to board the bus due to leave at 10pm on April 19. And I didn't have to wait long for it to happen in reality.

The man directly in front of me, as I attempted to board the bus, was engaged in hand-to-hand combat with the driver, whilst screaming, "I need tae get tae London tae see ma faither!" Mercifully, after a minute or two of struggling, the driver won the battle and ejected him forcefully from the bus. As I had a valid ticket and opted not to exhibit any outwardly violent behaviour, I was allowed on without incident. I shoved my travel bag into the rack, took a window seat and off we went to London.

I would not recommend the bus to anyone if they can afford the train fare. It's cramped, full to capacity and takes around eight to nine hours to reach the destination. I eventually got off the damned thing at Victoria, having had next to no sleep and still with a Tube journey to complete before I could rest at my friend Clive's house in South London.

Clive is a mate from Edinburgh who kindly gave me permission to sleep on his sofa until I could find somewhere to live. I felt drained, but with my bag on my back, I made it to the Tube and arrived at Clive's house around 45 minutes later.

Here I was in my adopted home city with no job and so few possessions as to be able to fit them all into my travel bag, but I was glad of the breather. *This is nice*, I thought. *I can relax for the rest of the day, knowing I made it to London safely.* I have no idea what exactly happened next, but knew I felt decidedly groggy and in a state of semi-consciousness. Weirder still, I appeared to be on a stretcher and being pushed into the back of an ambulance. I had never been in an ambulance before and it certainly wasn't on my tick-list of things to do on arrival in London.

The ambulance seemed to be moving but I didn't seem to have the ability to speak. So I was unable to inquire exactly why I was in it and not sitting on Clive's couch, the last place I remembered being. Most odd.

When I next regained consciousness, I was lying on a bed in what I later found out to be a hospital in Tooting. My only prior knowledge about Tooting was that it was the setting for the 1970's British sitcom *Citizen Smith*. But TV trivia, although a fine enough diversion, is not necessarily all that reassuring. The question still remained: How did I end up in a hospital bed in Tooting? That night, Clive helped me piece together the events that had unfolded.

Back to 9am, and I was sitting on the couch watching television while Clive sat on the floor drinking a cup of tea. I then rolled off the couch and on to the floor. Clive, however, took little interest in my behaviour, as he thought I was just mucking about.

It was only when I began to convulse violently that it became apparent all was not as it should be. At some point during the convulsions, I started to foam at the mouth. This is the point Clive thought it might be a good idea to phone for an ambulance. Obviously, the violent convulsions minus mouth foam were not enough to warrant emergency action to be taken, but luckily I had found Clive's tipping point.

It's true you have to up your game in London: the convulsions alone would not just have got me an ambulance in Edinburgh, but probably a police escort as well.

Anyway, it appeared that the call to the emergency service was a worthwhile one as, no sooner had I started to foam at the mouth, then I literally began to turn blue.

I had no idea what was going on at this point, but Clive was scared witless and longing for the sound of a siren and flashing lights before he had to explain why there was a dead body in his flat.

They didn't take long to appear, I was informed later, and it was as they were bundling me into the thing that I was briefly aware something, albeit something I had no understanding of, had happened.

I eventually came to my senses some hours later in a hospital bed. I still had no idea what had occurred and so asked to see a doctor. To his credit, the doctor appeared almost immediately, a bit like the shopkeeper in *Mr Benn*, only with a medical degree. He told me what had happened, aided by the fact that Clive told him what he had witnessed.

The doctor asked me if I suffered from epilepsy. *Epilepsy?* I told him that I've never suffered from any disease, and I'm definitely not epileptic. He moved a bit closer and said in hushed tones: "I'm going to ask you a question and it will go no further – did you take any drugs last night?"

I told him that all I did the night before was sit uncomfortably on a bus for eight to nine hours with no drug intake whatsoever. I was pleased I could answer the question with a clean conscience, but before I could take any moral high ground, I noticed that walking towards me were my father and brother. This was all getting very strange indeed. Perhaps I had been taking drugs and they were a hallucination?

Unbeknown to me, Clive had phoned them, and they had panicked and got on the first train to London (no bus for them, wisely). I later found out that my mother was at work and there was no time to waste by worrying her.

It was at this point that I began to suffer from the double whammy of hunger pains and acute embarrassment. I hadn't eaten for some time but, luckily, the doctor seemed intent on making sure I got some food – sausage and chips with a can of Coke. It's a child's dinner but it tasted mighty good.

Sadly, there was no such remedy for the humiliation I felt. Not even 24 hours had passed since I'd said my goodbyes to family and friends in Edinburgh and embarked on my life-changing adventure. This was it: I was leaving Scotland to find a better life, and I wouldn't see anyone back home until I had proved my worth in the sprawling metropolis of London, where after much hard work and toil I would be a self-made success.

Instead, I was lying in a hospital bed, looking like a panda – because all the blood vessels around my eyes had burst, due to the intensity of the convulsions – eating sausage and chips, while my father and brother wondered what exactly had happened since they'd last seen me some 14 hours previously. It's a question no one could find a conclusive answer to and, indeed, never did.

All I do know is that I was very lucky. If Clive hadn't been there, I could easily have swallowed my tongue and choked to death, according to the doctor. I liked it better when he was asking me if I fancied some sausage and chips, to be honest.

There could just as easily have been complications

connected to me turning blue and foaming at the mouth, but I was barely listening to his explanation by this point. I was feeling very dazed and had just noticed my reflection – and struggled to comprehend that the person staring back with two apparent black eyes was, in fact, me. 'What an entrance to London this has been,' I thought to myself – certainly more of an initial impact than Dick Whittington had, but admittedly without the literary legacy. I'll give the guy his due though, that Whittington was certainly a maverick: most people wait until they've got a place of their own before getting a cat.

I had to go for a series of scans in subsequent weeks and months to determine a cause for what happened. I was booked in to various hospitals and specialist surgeries to find what exactly was wrong with my brain, as something had clearly gone haywire, neurologically speaking. The strange thing is, in as much as it's slightly worrying to find out you may have a brain default, I was far less stressed than I probably should have been. At least I had appointments to fill up my diary, albeit nothing in the way of work bookings. It felt good to wake up in the morning and actually have somewhere I was meant to be at a particular time.

I would rather it was a meeting about potential work opportunities at BBC Television Centre or Channel 4's headquarters, but at least I was getting out of the house, whether it be Clive's place in South London or the flatshare I subsequently moved into in Kentish Town, North London, three weeks after my hospitalisation.

I really didn't mind going to the neurological section of the hospital in Roehampton, South London, or any of the other specialist places I was sent to. In some instances, I was told to lie down before being backed into a huge brain scanner, by way of a high-tech conveyor belt. I wouldn't recommend this to anyone prone to bouts of claustrophobia, as the whole body ends up in a big, white tunnel while the scans are taken.

On another occasion, I was sent to a specialist in Richmond, where a multitude of electrodes were attached to my head and what looked like a very state-of-the-art hairdryer – the kind you only get in pricey salons – did circuits of my head. At times, I almost forgot that these and several other processes were being undertaken to determine why I convulsed so violently that April morning, as it was all rather relaxing. But, in the end, all results came back inconclusively.

It appeared that it was simply a freak occurrence, albeit one which could have killed me. Some specialists said it may have been brought on by the cramped conditions of the bus, others that it may have had something to do with subconscious stress.

The only finding they could all come to, with some element of certainty, was that I wasn't suffering from epilepsy. That was fine by me, and with that knowledge I felt I could put the whole episode firmly in the past. Still though, hell of an entrance to my newly adopted home town.

3

LOST IN TRANSMISSION

Nobody likes a name-dropper so let's get this out of the way quickly. I have met some very famous people in my line of work, ranging from Johnny Depp and James Brown, to Angelina Jolie and Leonardo DiCaprio. Many such meetings require you to hit the ground running, as time constraints at a junket or film premiere are extremely tight and, as a result, it's hard to get a feel for the person behind the celebrity mask.

There will be more about that in a later chapter, but the instances that stick with me most are those odder occasions, sometimes even when there are no cameras around.

Wikipedia and I

The internet is a very handy thing indeed. It has made all our lives better but in the wrong hands can make them worse. Here is one example. My flatmate at the time had an interesting hobby for a while. It would involve drinking wine and adding details to my Wikipedia page, a page set up by someone unknown to me.

Also unknown to me was that my flatmate was doing this, until it was mentioned live on BBC radio in my presence, quite matter of factly, that as a 12-year-old child, I had appeared in the video for the Russ Abbot smash hit, 'Atmosphere' (alas, I was eight when the song came out and nowhere near the video shoot).

I could only deny the story, whilst inside my head the voice of Withnail was screaming, 'Al, you terrible c**t!' Thankfully, I didn't opt to say that out loud, although if proof were needed of the direct correlation between wine, a couch, a broadband connection, a Wikipedia password and live national radio, it was there and then.

Sadly, not everyone had tuned in to hear my public denial. I received phone calls and texts from various excited friends and acquaintances, all saying they had no idea I had appeared in the video. These same people had been noticeably less impressed when I told them about the world-famous actors, directors and musicians I had actually met and interviewed. It just goes to show that people are generally weird, but with an internet connection, they are also dangerous.

The Newsround Knock-Back

I was once invited to something called a BBC Contributors Party, where the great and the good of BBC on-screen talent are in attendance. The drink is free and with that the chances of booze-fuelled embarrassment raised. Having chatted to a few people throughout the night, I noticed that a female presenter from *Newsround* was in attendance, who I had a slight fancy for.

Here is the strange thing. Everyone has innocent fancies for people they see on the TV. It's all perfectly innocent because, in all likelihood, they will never meet them – but here I was in a position to do just that. It was in the latter stages of the evening when I had my 'carpe diem' moment (which was definitely aided by my intake of free red wine). As I noticed her readying to leave, I took it as my chance to ask her out on a date, safe in the knowledge that if I didn't, I would wake up the next morning and bemoan the wasted opportunity.

I calmly walked up to her, introduced myself and asked if she would like to go for a drink sometime in the near future. I hardly had time to get this all out before she was telling me why she couldn't. With a smile and a sympathetic look, she told me she would have loved to but was already seeing someone and, with that, I instigated a quick goodbye and retreated back into the main body of people, with the aim of finding more free wine to cushion the blow.

I woke the next morning, glad that I had gone for it, embarrassed that I had suffered the knock-back, but relieved that we didn't move in the same social circles. The only way I would ever see her again, I reasoned, would be at a similar function, where preparations could be made for such an encounter, like drinking free wine to curb the embarrassment. I quickly forgot about it all and got on with my business.

A week later, I made my way to Acton in West London to see two friends – a couple who lived in a nice flat on a terraced street not too far from the overground. I had spent some great nights there in the past, listening to music, having a laugh and eating good food. As I walked down their road though, my heart sank and a mixture of nausea and dread permeated through my stomach. It was the *Newsround* girl, walking in the front door which led to my friends' place. This was most alarming. Why on earth was she here? Why was I now hiding behind a white van trying to compose myself? What if she was to see me and think I was stalking her? There were too many questions going unanswered...

I made my way over the road, rang the bell and, when I got into the flat, was relieved to see that she was nowhere to be seen. Unless it was all part of an elaborate set-up to get us together, as she had seen the error of her ways? It wasn't, as it turned out, as my friends informed me she had moved into the flat downstairs.

What were the chances of that? The size of London, the number of streets – this was incredible. She had moved in with her boyfriend, and they were really happy together, apparently. Good for them, but shame that I had to now find some new friends or persuade my present ones to move house. That would be a tricky task, I wagered.

I would continue to see my friends who lived in that house, but it was with obvious trepidation. The very next time I visited, I wore a hat, but thankfully such a disguise was superfluous, as she was nowhere to be seen. The next time, however, she was getting out of her car as I approached minus headgear. I took refuge behind a large recycling bin, crouching whilst untying and then re-tying my shoelace, in an effort to appear less conspicuous.

Thankfully, and not before another occasion had me stalling behind a white van on the other side of the road until she had found her keys and disappeared through the main door – long enough for me to make my way over, safe in the knowledge there wouldn't be a crossover, I was dealt a huge stroke of luck. My friends announced they were expecting their first child. What utterly wonderful news this was, as it meant they would have to move to a bigger house with a garden.

The miracle of a new life was one thing, but the pleasure of visiting a house without having to hide or wear a disguise was another. I have never felt such relief as a direct result of procreation. I also vowed not to approach a woman with romantic intentions again, unless I was sure she lived in a different city to me.

Cricket and Caledonians

There was the time when I was asked to make some short films with the England cricket team to coincide with the Ashes series of 2009. The project was funded by the then England team sponsor, Vodafone. As well as detailing the history of the Ashes series, I would be given unprecedented access to the team.

This was a great opportunity to learn the finer aspects of the sport from the players themselves and involved filming at every single Ashes test match.

I saw myself as a modern-day version of A.G. Macdonell's protagonist in the 1933 novel *England, Their England*, especially the chapter all about a village cricket match. I too was a Scot, viewing the English in their uniquely English habitat and with it all their quirks and eccentricities. A stranger in a strange land, if you will – but all the time in the middle of a hugely iconic sporting occasion.

Not that anyone at Vodafone gave a toss about that, of course. It was a chance for them to flex their commercial muscle, by enlisting the whole England team to be part of a series of short films that helped promote their brand name to the online audience. Whatever the reasoning, the finished films were both well-made and well-received.

If I were to take away some lessons from the whole thing, they would be: The more you learn about cricket the more interesting it becomes; that it is almost impossible to see a fast ball coming at you from a professional bowler; and that Kevin Pietersen appears to have little in the way of a sense of humour.

L-Plates and Lies

I'm not into cars and never have been, but when I was asked to front a motoring-based show, it was a no-brainer. It was to be a spin-off from *Top Gear*, to be more precise, a special they did for Comic Relief called *Stars In Fast Cars*, a spin-off itself from the *Star In A Reasonably Priced Car* feature.

The premise was a simple one: four celebrities would compete over a series of motoring challenges to see who would be crowned that week's Star In A Fast Car.

The celebrities involved included Olympians Sir Steve Redgrave and Jonathan Edwards, TV chef Ainsley Harriott, BBC royal correspondent Jennie Bond and comedian and impressionist Jon Culshaw. A random mix, granted. We filmed 10 shows, which originally went out on BBC3, before transferring to BBC1. There was just one snag though – I couldn't drive.

It wasn't even a case of having the basics of driving under my belt, but just not having got round to getting a licence – in fact, I had never in my life attempted to drive a car. Not a clue. Due to this, a deal was struck that the BBC would splash out for some lessons and I would pay for some others out of my own pocket. So I could then take a test and pass it before the show went to air.

The only problem was that it turned out I was an awful driver. I didn't seem to have what millions of others possess when it comes to taking the wheel. Something in my head just didn't compute and even the simplest of manoeuvres was an absolute headache.

After around 12 lessons, my instructor had to break it to me that I was nowhere near ready to take a test. He would also break it to me that he was having an extra-marital affair because, as someone who didn't smoke or drink, he had to have some fun in his life. It was fuzzy logic, but at least he could drive.

Here was I, on the other hand, filming a show about driving, whilst lying through my teeth to the celebrity guests, who invariably asked me if I got to have a go at driving the Ferrari or whatever the car was. My pre-prepared answer was that due to health-and-safety concerns, I was forbidden to do so. This worked temporarily, but I knew time was running out before I was really in the soup.

There were around two months between the filming being completed and going to air, during which time I continued to have as many lessons as I could before the test, which was due to take place a week before the first show going out. When the day of reckoning came, I made my way to the Mill Hill test centre in North London, took the test and failed. *Shit.* All I could think of doing was to take more lessons and re-book a test as soon as I could.

The big problem was that the show would now be on television and I would be driving around with a huge, sodding triangle on the roof. Alongside the stress of figuring out how to drive, I could now add paranoia to the mix. What if people recognised me? Would the BBC receive complaints? Would I have to defend my professional integrity? Would anyone give a shit in the first place?

Well, as far as I know, it was all kept under wraps, but that didn't stop a car full of lads heralding me as the presenter of "that show with the cars in it", as I pulled up to traffic lights at the top of Finchley Road – which, incidentally, is a fairly terrifying road to drive along when not having a clear idea how driving works in the first place.

Anyway, one of the lads noticed me driving and quickly told his other mate in the front passenger street. Then the two in the back found out and, before long, there were four guys banging on their windows before rolling them down to point, wave and then sing a song to the tune of 'Guantanamera' with the lyrics: *You from the telly. It's only you from the telly.* All this and I still had to concentrate on not stalling the car. I bet this never happened to Clarkson.

In hindsight, it may have helped with my motivation to conquer my fear of driving, as I did pass my test second time around. I was losing around a stone in sweat after every nightmare lesson, not to mention haemorrhaging money in the process. It was as much about relief as celebration that day. I shook the adjudicator's hand and then that of my instructor, who was at the test centre awaiting my news. I then asked if my instructor would drive me home, which he did. I haven't driven a car since.

Flugging Cheek

The biggest live audience I have ever played to was 80,000 in Hyde Park, London – and it wasn't a time for political jokes, it was a fun day out for the masses. I had been filming a show for Channel 4 called the *Red Bull Air Race*, which, as the title suggests, was an air race sponsored by Red Bull. It took place all around the world and was certainly a great gig to be doing.

At the same time, there was a huge event taking place in Hyde Park called the 'Flugtag', which consisted of contestants making their own flying machines and seeing how far they could travel off a huge ramp before landing in the Serpentine. This was not *University Challenge*, but I believe some of the participants may have been students.

It was a long day's filming in the summer heat and, during downtime, there were two DJs employed to keep the crowd 'up' and 'lively'. They did this by mainly using call-and-response methods, such as "Are you having a good time?" to which the crowd would respond with cheers. This seemed to go on for a long time, with every question eliciting the same response of cheering from the crowd.

I decided to have a go myself at one stage, but with a slight deviation. Here's what I said:

Me – "Give me a cheer if you're enjoying the sunshine!"

Crowd – Cheers

Me – "Give me a cheer if you're enjoying the show!"

Crowd – Cheers

Me – "Give me a cheer if you think [then Prime Minister] Gordon Brown is fit to run the country!"

Crowd – Cheers/confusion/muffled clapping/producer panic.

The producer didn't know how to take it. But as we were about to start filming again, had no time to reprimand me even if he had wanted to. I wasn't out of the woods yet, though. Throughout the day, the DJs had been referring to the two huge banks of spectators around the Serpentine as the north bank and the south bank. Along the lines of "North bank, give us a cheer! South bank, give us a cheer!" Fair enough, but I thought we could run with it more. I was asked to do a link which would also show us the sheer numbers watching that day and would also be heard over the massive PA system.

No problem, I thought to myself, and here's what I came out with: "There's a huge number of spectators here today. We have the north bank (cue huge cheers); we have the south bank (cue more huge cheers)." I then looked straight at the camera and added: "Alas, at the moment, we have yet to find out how the Flugtag experience is going down with the people on the West Bank. We can only hope favourably." This didn't go down well with the producer either, who made it clear there was no way we could use that in the show, as the Flugtag and continuing Israel/Palestine crisis had no crossover potential.

Only the 80,000 people in attendance ever heard the non-censored version, but that was still 20,000 more than were in attendance at the 2014 Champions League Final. One of them was broadcaster and writer Danny Baker, who I later found out that day loved the line. I was happy to please.

There was one final twist that day, long after everyone had left the park. I had been invited to a wedding but, due to that day's filming, was only able to make it to the evening reception. When I got there, the groom, knowing full well I was accustomed to public speaking, asked if I would announce that an evening menu of food would be served imminently.

To be honest, all I wanted was a drink and a bit peace but of course I obliged. Little did I know that two spectators from that afternoon's Flugtag were also invited to the evening reception, and were duly impressed when they discovered that the bloke fronting the whole Hyde Park show had also been employed by the groom, Paul, to tell them when the food was ready. This time, I didn't even try to make any political jokes – after all, I wasn't even being paid.

From that day forth, I swore never to mix politics and performance ever again. This self-imposed sanction came in handy when, in the run up to the 2014 referendum vote on Scottish independence, I was asked by the Better Together side to voiceover a film for them in an increased media campaign to persuade people to vote 'No' and thus preserve the United Kingdom. I declined the offer, even though the money would have been handy – but sanctions were in place.

Furthermore, I disagreed with the campaign and was actually in the 'Yes' camp for Scottish independence, so it would have gone completely against my principles. As it turned out, the 'No' camp didn't need my help anyway, as they won the vote with a 55–45% majority. Still, I was left with a clear conscience, if not an independent country to call my homeland. The fact that, at the end of the week, I was invited on BBC Radio 5Live show *The Manifesto* to discuss the result (and thus had the chance to satirically lambast my least favourite Westminster politicians) was highly satisfying but, sadly, of little consequence or reward in the grand scheme of things – but the fact that the producer, on this occasion, was definitely in favour of political jocularity was, however, rather pleasing.

4

SANITY AND ARTISTIC ADVANCEMENT

I was making short films, playing in bands and generally striving to be creative, long before I ever worked in broadcasting. The reason I got a TV job in the first place was a mixture of the two, really. I started to make videos to accompany songs my friends and I had written. This naturally progressed to making stand-alone short films, one of which I sent to the BBC – which got me a job. I've continued to make short films ever since, and for two main reasons: sanity and artistic advancement.

I have always had the urge to 'create' and manifest the ideas floating around in my head. Not to at least try to do something with them would, for me, make everyday life turgid and unfulfilling. Also, I found that if, at times, I wasn't attaining artistic fulfilment in my professional work, I could find creative satisfaction from my independent projects instead.

I think this is why I identify so much with figures such as cult comic-book writer Harvey Pekar, who, despite not reaching the pinnacle of commercial success, had a strong desire to write and create art. I have also, from time to time, believed that some of my ideas had the potential to lead to bigger projects, such as a TV series or feature film. At the very least, I believed they could show my versatility as a writer, performer and director.

The short I sent to the BBC that bagged me my first TV job was called *Getting Out The House* – about what you can get up to in the summer if you are skint – an autobiographical tale, for sure. It was seen by Stuart Murphy, who would go on to be controller of BBC Three and Director of Sky Entertainment Channels. He liked what he saw, invited me down to London and, on meeting me, offered me a presenting job on the now-defunct digital music channel UK Play. It was as straightforward as that. He also asked if I had an agent but I had to tell him that, when you are working as an insurance temp in an office in a business park on the outskirts of Edinburgh, there isn't much call for artist management. He would later fix me up with my first agent.

I soon found out that this was not a typical entry into the world of television, as the other presenters I met seemed to be either ex-models or ex-researchers, desperate to appear in front of camera. Undeterred, I kept making all sorts of films.

These included a promo video to accompany a song I co-wrote with my friend Milo called 'Columbo & Coffee', all about our favourite TV detective, as well as two epic kung-fu movies. The first of which, *Fist Of Fernandez*, was shown on the digital channel BBC Choice. As a result, we were paid £50 for the privilege and thus given a budget for a follow-up. That turned out to be *Fist Of Fernandez 2: The School Of the Six High Noons*, in which I reprised my role as the evil Tango Fernandez, who had fought his nemesis, Billy Lopez, in the first film and, in the sequel, his younger brother, Junior Lopez. My character had been successful in defeating the elder Lopez sibling, with help from his henchman and part-time chef, Bad Bradley Hot Wok. Alas, there was no such luck in the sequel, where Lopez Jr took his and his family's revenge.

The film is also notable for featuring the then President Of The United States, Bill Clinton, in one of the scenes. As my co-director John started filming the sequel when he was in New York City on holiday, it coincided with a visit from the Leader Of The Free World, whom John got on camera when his motorcade passed through a Manhattan street. To my knowledge, it remains the only kung-fu movie to include a US president.

Around the same time, I also made my polemic short film *The Anti–Fantastic Campaign*, which, as the title suggests, was about the overuse of the word 'fantastic' in British broadcasting, and which I would come back to years later in *The Anti–Fantastic Campaign: A Retrospective*.

Due to a complete non-existence of funding for such filmic undertakings, I would simply borrow bog-standard cameras and rely on people giving up their time for free. This was fine in theory but, on more than one occasion, would involve people turning up drunk or stoned. As they had been kind enough to work for free, I couldn't berate them, no matter how much I wanted to.

Having said that, I don't remember too much drunkenness on set for *In Search Of Jimmy Nail*, a spoof documentary attempting to track down the Geordie actor. I do, however, recall many drinks after wrapping, due to the multitude of Newcastle Brown Ale cans, which had been bought as props.

The first short I did after moving to London was called *Absolute Rhubarb* and featured myself taking to the streets in search of celebrities, who would be placed on a league table to find out who was best. They would be ranked using my KLF theory: K for the kudos of the person, L for their level of fame and F for their friendliness. I was lucky enough to enlist actor and comedian Peter Serafinowicz, whom I literally bumped into in Soho. Peter duly won the competition, not only because he received the highest score, but also because he was the one celebrity I met that day.

I wasn't restricted to filming in London though. I had a pal with a good camera who lived in Hastings, on the south coast. If I wanted to enlist both himself and the camera for my short, *The Skills Of Conversation*, I would have to travel south. This I did and it was worth it. The film was all about the techniques people could utilise in order to make them better conversationalists, in a world increasingly taken over by impersonal modern technologies. Particular attention was paid to a technique called the Heartburn Pause, in which a person pretends to have heartburn halfway through a sentence, in order to buy some time to recall exactly what it is they wanted to be saying coherently.

The filming was to be done over a day, but it was touch and go whether it would be completed before we had even begun. On arrival, my mate told me he was going through a rough patch with his wife and that things could get a bit uncomfortable over the course of the weekend. Nobody wants to be in the middle of a domestic when there are shorts to film. I have never wanted to get the job done and get back to London quite as much before, or since. Thankfully, after bagging the final shot I was on the first available train back to Victoria.

Another trip to the south coast saw me filming a prelude to a stage show I was doing in London, which consisted of esoteric and entertaining clips of films, documentaries and musical performances being shown and discussed before an audience.

I thought I would also film something especially for the show, a minute-and-a-half offering called *Stage Fit*, which basically consisted of shots of me getting fit for stage performance. Everything went swimmingly, until I unwittingly ventured on to the nudist area of Brighton beach and unsettled some of the naturalists by running as fast as I could, dressed in a running vest and shorts, screaming at the top of my voice, "Life Fit, Stage Fit, Yeeeesssssss!!!" This seemed to upset them greatly, but more upsetting was the sight of some of those bodies, which simply did not warrant being shown off in their entirety on what was a chilly summer's morn.

Perhaps it was due to this invasion of the nudists that returning to a studio location became more favourable and, indeed, an imperative for *The 3 Minute Chat Show*, my next opus.

It was a pretty big undertaking, consisting of set designers, studio, cameramen, sound recordists, audience and even make-up. Quite the crew, but when you intend to completely revolutionise a traditional entertainment format, high production values – or at least the best production values you can muster – are absolutely of the essence.

The show took all the major aspects of a chat show, such as topicality, a sidekick (comedian and actor David Reed), guest (Miles Jupp) and musical act (Allo Darlin'), and condensed it into three minutes. My aim was to keep it entertaining whilst completely eradicating the flab – brevity being the key. I was very happy with the results and felt it ticked all the boxes, and that I had done a really good job as writer, performer, director and producer. Everyone I showed it to loved it, as well. It seemed it was just those from the main UK TV channels who were somewhat apathetic towards it. I thought it was a no-brainer for TV companies to utilise as online content, but that wasn't to be the case. Nevertheless, it still worked as a stand-alone piece and, if you had a spare five minutes to fill in your day, you could watch it and still have a couple of minutes to do whatever you saw fit.

On Creativity and Ambition

It's worth pointing out that creativity and ambition are not necessarily comfortable bedfellows. Every time I start a project, I do so for artistic reasons, but then thoughts slip in of the commercial opportunities, which can often lead to disappointment.

If one were to keep just artistic ambitions, then there would be only gratification from a job well done, but it's easy to become too ambitious or just unrealistic. The fact is that the demand may simply not exist for what it is you feel inspired to do. Although, at these times, it can be easy to wonder why you ever undertake such creative dalliances when they result in no financial gain, at the very least you are doing something, and not just talking about it.

I've always believed in just getting out and filming, as opposed to procrastinating about stuff but never doing anything. I've met people over the years who seem to think they are following a Bukowski-esque approach to creativity, that is, they get drunk and talk about what they are going to do artistically but never get around to actually doing it. The thing is, Charles got drunk but never forgot to write.

If you get off your arse, at the very least you can be criticised for doing something as opposed to being criticised for doing nothing. Very rarely are the bone idle celebrated, although there seem to be some members of the royal family who are trotted out on state occasions, seemingly to milk the public acclaim for services even they must surely be completely unaware of themselves providing.

It is obviously gratifying to undertake a project, see it through to the end, be happy with the results and for it to do you some favours in the future, as well. My short film *Timber!* (detailed in full in Chapter 15) is a case in point. Not only was the film shown in the USA and Europe via a distribution deal with Shorts International (which ended up with me making some money in royalties), it was also the reason I made my debut on the prestigious BBC Radio 4 weekday 6.30pm slot.

Radio 4's *It's Not What You Know* was a comedy panel show, ably hosted by *Timber!* cast member, the aforementioned Miles Jupp, and featured comedians, writers and broadcasters competing against each other.

It was recorded at the BBC Radio Theatre in central London.

To his credit, Miles was keen to have me on but the producer seemed unaware of my work, regardless of the fact that by that point I had chalked up over 50 appearances on the BBC Radio 5Live Sony Gold-winning show *Fighting Talk* by basically being funny and informative, exactly what the Radio 4 programme required. Not to worry though, within a day of Miles showing him *Timber!*, I was booked to appear. Not only that, I won it as well. If only I had known that was the key to getting on Radio 4, I would have sent *Fist Of Fernandez* to the *Today* programme years before.

5

CELEBRITY AND AUTHENTICITY

Playing the celebrity game is a risky business, as it seems you can very easily be up one minute and down the next. I have never taken any of it that seriously, which I must point out has never been the case with the work itself.

I've never had a problem being around celebrities in a professional context but I tend not to hang about with them socially. This is probably down to the fact I don't really know many of them well enough. Many of my friends have nothing to do with show business and, those who do, tend to be from the behind-the-camera faculty: directors, editors, sound recordists, that type of thing.

This is not to say that I do not feel comfortable or enjoy the company of other performers or those in the public eye – in fact, far from it. Several occasions spring to mind, such as when I was appearing at *The Telegraph*'s literary festival, where I was in conversation with Miles

Jupp about his book, *Fibber In The Heat*, in which I make a brief cameo.

Note to readers: As you will see, there is more than one mention of Miles in this book. To clarify, all mentions of Miles refer to my friend and collaborator, the comedian and actor, Miles Jupp, although I can think of at least two other Mileses with whom I have also worked and who were sterling fellows. I have yet to meet a bad Miles, but have met both good and bad Tobys, Jeremys and Justins.

Mingling With The Literati

Miles and I have done quite a few festivals together on the topic of *Fibber In The Heat* but also broadened the discussion out, in order to discuss all manner of topics. The audiences certainly seemed to enjoy themselves, if the laughter and applause were anything to go by. The great thing is, at these events, I have met interesting people who have immediately garnered my respect.

Book festivals are also hugely different from music festivals, of which I have also attended my own fair share, both as a presenter and as a spectator. At music festivals such as Scotland's T In The Park, many spectators – not to mention those performing – are strung out on all manner of intoxicants and can be a danger to themselves, let alone others. The literary festival, while still selling alcohol, is a far more relaxed affair with absolutely no need for a designated chill-out zone.

At *The Telegraph*'s Ways With Words festival, which took place at the beautiful Dartington Hall in Devon, we took to the stage in the main chamber directly after

Michael Palin, who had been in discussion about his new novel. I recall thinking at the time that it was a pretty strong support act.

Later on that evening, I would sit around a dinner table with not just Palin but also Michael Buerk and John McCarthy. We chatted over a roast and I felt in esteemed company while holding my own, not awestruck but respectful.

We actually ended up getting drunk with John McCarthy in the bar afterwards, where Miles took it upon himself to invite John and myself round to his for a barbecue at some point in the near future.

It was only when John went to the toilet that Miles turned to me and in hushed tones confessed, "I don't know why I did that: I don't own a barbecue." I suppose it shows we can all get a bit carried away with alcohol and ex-hostages for company. I'm just thankful Terry Waite wasn't there: the thought of him being invited on a caravan holiday, only to find out nobody owned a mobile home, would have been devastating.

Another literary festival we appeared at was in Wales at Laugharne. The first person I met there, and who was also appearing, was Nick Drake's producer Joe Boyd, and I thoroughly enjoyed telling him just how much I loved Drake's work.

Later on that evening, I would end up getting drunk with him, the author John Niven, writers and columnists Grace Dent and Caitlin Moran, musician Robyn Hitchcock, music journalist Pete Paphides, DJ and writer Stuart Maconie and former *The Word* magazine editor and music broadcaster, Mark Ellen.

My intention here isn't to namedrop for the sake of name-dropping however. Here were people that, unlike some minor celebrities, had, to my eyes at least, done worthwhile things, written books, were interesting to talk to and obviously passionate about their work – people I would like to think of as kindred spirits. They were also welcoming and let us have as much of their booze as we wanted, which was greatly appreciated.

Man's Best Friend: Crufts and Clare Balding

While there may be something of a dichotomy between being famous and staying genuine, I do believe it's possible to be famous, kind, interesting and at the top of your game, all at the same time. I had the great pleasure of working with Clare Balding at, of all places, Crufts. I was asked to go there, if I may use the words of Channel 4, "in a Louis Theroux-esque capacity" and file daily reports that would be played out on the Channel 4 show covering the event, which was presented by Clare.

I saw it as an unusual event with great comic potential, and that proved to be the case. It was also an opportunity to witness, at close hand, Clare's work, and what was quickly evident was that her mixture of knowledge and personableness was second to none.

When she stole the show on the TV coverage for the 2012 London Olympics, I made sure I emailed to congratulate her on a job brilliantly done, and she replied immediately with thanks and gracious modesty. Whenever television is accused of dumbing down, it's good to know there are still those with intelligence to stem the flow, and few can match Clare.

After The Evans

A more complex character I worked with, and probably even more well-known, is Chris Evans. I presented the spin-off for the game show he produced for Channel 4, *Boys and Girls*. Somewhat unprecedentedly, the show I did garnered good reviews but the main one didn't fare as well, leaving me in the strange and frustrating position of having delivered the goods and won plaudits, but being unable to do it all again when the main show failed to be recommissioned.

It was, however, something of an honour to be picked by Chris Evans to host the show. There's no doubting he gave Nineties British television a much-needed kick up the arse, at least in the entertainment genre, with his ground-breaking shows *Don't Forget Your Toothbrush* and *TFI Friday*.

I was invited to his mansion once in Surrey to 'talk shop' and, as it was the first time I had been there, I decided to take a gift for him and his then-wife Billie Piper, as it is customary to do so. I would have done the same for someone living in a council flat in Leith, of course, and have done on numerous occasions.

Anyway, I opted to give them a vinyl copy of the soundtrack to the Peter Sellers film, *After The Fox*, the title tune of which is sung by Sellers and The Hollies, and is quite brilliant. The music is composed and conducted by Burt Bacharach, with Hal David providing the lyrics to the great title track. When I presented Chris with the record, he was rather taken aback and told me that nobody came to their house with gifts. *Good thing I do things differently*, I wagered.

I was also surprised when Chris told me he didn't read books, as he was obviously an intelligent person and there were books in the house. Perhaps he meant he didn't read that often or just not fiction? Who knows? Although, he would later go on to write two autobiographies himself. On another occasion, he discussed at length an Andy Kaufman biography with me, which he thought was a great work.

Whilst speaking about my love of the written word, I expressed at one stage a great admiration for *Catch-22*. A few weeks later, I received a Christmas present from Chris – an original poster for the *Catch-22* movie adaptation. This came as a total surprise and was a generous and thoughtful gift.

I also thought it was a superb case of present reciprocation – *Catch 22* original movie poster in exchange for the *After The Fox* soundtrack on heavyweight vinyl. For me, this is what showbiz relationships should be all about.

It wasn't a subject Chris and I spoke about at the time, but I do like the fact that the use of the book's title is now very much in the public domain as a well-used phrase, but was actually an invention by the book's author, Joseph Heller, as opposed to something already in existence.

A clever man indeed was Mr H and, while the film doesn't quite match up to the majesty of the book, it's still a damn fine poster to hang in a clip frame or indeed a made-to-measure oak frame, if you have the finances to spare.

The A-List

I have interviewed a great number of the A-list, as well as a sprinkling from the B's and C's, and once someone I believed to be a D. But she turned out simply to be a member of the public who was particularly well-dressed.

Regardless, I always strived to ensure the interview was something special and unique, even if we only had a short amount of time together. It was important to me, as I felt that an unexpected line of questioning would be a pleasant surprise for the interviewee and the viewer alike.

Admittedly, this wasn't always easy, especially when they had already been subjected to hundreds, or in some cases thousands, of interviews throughout their careers. I saw it as a worthy challenge though, with preparation of utmost importance. I would focus on doing my research and find out as much as I could about the person I was interviewing.

For the most part, these encounters took place at either pre-arranged junkets or at award ceremonies such as the BAFTAs. To many journalists or broadcasters, these were rather frustrating occasions where you were lucky if you got a few minutes with someone. However, I saw it as, not just an exciting challenge, but a way to cut out the fluff and get to the interesting questions. In a way, it was a harbinger of *The 3 Minute Chat Show*, whereby I got straight to the meat of the matter.

The thing was, the A-List seemed to be as desperate for an unusual line of questioning as I was keen to deliver it – and I often ended up being asked to stay for longer by the likes of Johnny Depp and George Clooney. They seemed to view me as a breath of fresh air and I was happy to oblige. Perhaps this was because I knew what I was talking about film-wise, having always done my research beforehand. Add to that my humour, which I used in the natural way I would with anyone else, famous or not.

Perhaps, the greatest example of the interviewer/interviewee enjoyment pact was sealed on my first trip to New York for a series of junkets and film screenings. This really was like being in a fantasy world, as I had recently signed off the dole after having bagged a job with Channel 4, who had arranged and paid for the trip. I was in dreamland but still focused on the interviews, and what a joy it was. I interviewed amongst others, the aforesaid George Clooney, plus Edward Norton, Catherine Zeta-Jones, Sam Rockwell and Spike Lee.

Aside from talking about the films they were appearing in, I did as I always do: strayed off topic and spoke about other films, and generally used deviation as a device to make things more interesting. This certainly worked, and I even had Ed Norton intent on telling me how much he loved hill climbing in Scotland and the hotel he stayed in whilst in Edinburgh.

There were other actors in the hotel that I was informed I wouldn't be interviewing, such as Renée Zellweger. I actually had a couple of weeks before in London and we had got on really well. However, I was told by some kind of publicist (the type who always seem to have a clipboard, but no idea what their top five films would be) that, as I had interviewed her in London, there wasn't the time to do so in New York.

This seemed daft, as she was in a room directly off the hotel corridor where I was holding the interviews. Well, I thought, I haven't come all this way, and dressed up, just for a knock-back. I was in a smart pinstripe suit, shirt and tie, looking suitably Mod-esque. I felt this look made me appear smart, serious and ready for business. I also felt comfortable wearing it as it was my normal attire.

I told the publicist in polite and direct terms that she should inform Renée that I was outside and wanted to interview her. Within a minute, I was sitting in front of Renée, being miked up, with her saying it was great to see her 'friend' again. She was a total sweetheart although, I have to say, we 'friends' haven't got together since. I suppose those are the realities of a 'showbiz relationship'.

After a while, I once again decided to employ the critique I had already used in my short film *Absolute Rhubarb*, where I would rate the celebrities I'd met using my KLF theory: K – for the kudos of the person; L – for the level of fame they had and F – for how friendly they were. I even compiled an end-of-season league table at one point. The results as shown in that original rudimentary table were as follows:

The Absolute Rhubarb Champions League Of Film Stars Final Placings

1.	Renée Zellweger (US)	**28pts (Champion)**
2.	Johnny Depp (US)	27pts
3.	Jamie Lee Curtis (US)	26pts
4.	= Michael Caine (GB)	25pts
4.	= Will Smith (US)	25pts
6.	= Jim Carrey (CAN)	24pts
6.	= Edward Norton (US)	24pts
8.	Meg Ryan (US)	23pts
9.	= George Clooney (US)	22pts
9.	= Harrison Ford (US)	22pts
11.	= Paul Bettany (GB)	21pts
11.	= Samuel L Jackson (US)	21pts
11.	= Mark Ruffalo (US)	21pts
11.	= Arnold Schwarzenegger (US)	21pts
15.	Minnie Driver (GB)	20pts
16.	Orlando Bloom (GB)	19pts

Read in to that what you will, stats fans. I must say though, that at the time of writing, I would have Ruffalo much higher as, not only was he a great guy, but a damn fine actor. They all played their part, though, and went on to rebuild for the following season. I may post the detailed breakdown online some day but, to give some indication, here's a quick overview of my findings, based on being in people's company for a few minutes – and not just the ones from the first-ever league table:

- Leonardo DiCaprio – a proper actor and film star with the requisite chat
- Minnie Driver – a good laugh and a friendly soul
- Michael Caine – assured and approachable

- Johnny Depp – friendly, inquisitive and conversational
- Will Smith – professionally friendly and jovial
- Jim Carrey – live wire and interesting
- Harrison Ford – hard work and akin to getting blood out of a stone
- Arnold Schwarzenegger – chatty enough but lacking in substance
- Meg Ryan – delightful and funny
- Mark Ruffalo – personable, affable and, no doubt, punctual to boot
- Renée Zellweger – fun, friendly and down to earth
- Sam Rockwell – cool, friendly and laid–back
- Samuel L Jackson – a tad dull but friendly enough
- Tom Hanks – assured
- Paul Bettany – friendly and interesting
- Meryl Streep – classy, yet understated
- Angelina Jolie – affable and up for conversation
- Edward Norton – genuinely interesting
- Orlando Bloom – good-looking and playing to his strengths
- Jamie Lee Curtis – funny and entertaining
- Anjelica Huston – warm and motherly
- Cate Blanchett – intelligent, sharp and witty

My only regret is that I never met Jeff Goldblum. The occasions when I got slightly longer face-to-face time than the usual 5 minutes or less were few and far between, so when I presented a 45-minute TV special on the Wes Anderson film *The Life Aquatic With Steve Zissou*, it felt like I'd won a competition. Sadly, Bill Murray didn't make the promotional trip to the UK but Anjelica Huston, Cate Blanchett and director Wes did. I always like talking to directors, as they never get enough time in the spotlight in my opinion – not that some of them want it, as I would wager many prefer to stay behind camera. As ever, I was wearing a suit, which seemed to please Wes greatly, as he was also in his. We talked about *The Life Aquatic*, his other films and our mutual love of music and fine tailoring.

I then spoke to the other cast members, and found Anjelica Huston to be warm, friendly and jovial and Cate Blanchett much the same, but lacking the 'motherly' quality Anjelica seemed to have in abundance. It was a great shame not to meet Bill Murray though.

Sticking on the Wes Anderson connection, I also thoroughly enjoyed hosting a series of BAFTA master classes, whereby I would spend an hour in front of a live audience, interviewing a prominent director or producer. These were joyous, as there was enough time to get into the detail of someone's career, plus the chance to elicit interesting stories about certain films and the industry in general. One particular favourite was when I interviewed Barry Mendel, who produced the Wes Anderson movies *Rushmore* and *The Royal Tenenbaums*, as well as *Munich*, *The Sixth Sense* and *Bridesmaids*. We spoke about how he came to be a producer, the films he worked on and the wider industry. We chatted for a whole hour – what a luxury that was.

It wasn't just film stars and film-makers, though. The musicians were piling up too. Admittedly, many weren't as well-known globally as certain names from the film fraternity but, in my book, they were just as important. Perhaps my strangest musical interview, however, was with the Godfather Of Soul, James Brown. To be honest, the job was done before it began. I was always going to be able to say I met and interviewed the great James Brown and, even better, it was played out on national television, on the BBC.

The interview took place in the artists' village at the T In The Park festival, and it was the only interview I conducted there that had a live audience consisting of all the other bands playing that day – such was their reverence to the great man. I was no different, and it was impossible not to think of defining moments, places and actions, such as the Apollo in Harlem, saving Boston from rioting in '68, *Rocky IV*, and even the scene in *The Commitments* when they watch him perform.

There I was being confronted with a bonafide icon – and his wife Tomi Rae Hynie. Now, this wouldn't have been a problem had James Brown not insisted that she sat in on the interview – on camera. I wasn't going to argue with the big guy but it did feel absurd. I interviewed James Brown, while a woman I had never seen before, his former dancer and now marriage partner, sat beside us both and said nothing, but all the time stared at us. Weird, but I suppose if you're James Brown, you can get away with almost anything, even tax evasion for quite a time.

The strangeness was compounded though by the fact that it was difficult to understand a word he said. He still had a strong Southern drawl and, with his increasing years, wasn't as coherent as he once was, and quite simply seemed happy to still be performing. That was good enough for me. I was happy enough just to shake his hand and ask him a few questions, regardless of what his answers were or, for that matter, the closeness in proximity of his wife and former dancer.

6

THE ALBUM AND ME – A LOVE STORY SET TO MUSIC

When I was asked to be a judge for the 2013 Scottish Album Of The Year Awards (which was won by RM Hubbert's *Thirteen Lost & Found*), I was honoured and excited in equal measure.

I was in esteemed company, as the panel included Turner Prize-winning artists, broadsheet journalists and musicians. There was certainly a wealth of talent to be judged, as Scotland has always punched above its weight in terms of what it has given to the world – and not just culturally.

As Winston Churchill once said, "Of all the small nations of this earth, perhaps only the ancient Greeks surpass the Scots in their contribution to mankind." I have to be honest, I don't know what opinions Winston had on albums – but, for me, they are still a very important art form.

On more than one occasion, I have gone out to buy an album but come home with three, sometimes without the one I had initially intended to buy. I love shopping for them, trailing around record shops, looking at the cover and tracklisting on the way home, and finally playing it.

I also tend to strike up conversations with those behind the till if they look friendly enough. One such encounter found me enthusing on the brilliant Flamin' Groovies album *Teenage Head* to the middle-aged owner of a store, who was clearly more into rockabilly, if his hairstyle and clothing were anything to go by.

Thankfully, with the original vinyl hanging on the wall, he too clearly had great respect for one of the best records of 1971 – a year not shy of great album releases, which included *Sticky Fingers*, *Histoire de Melody Nelson*, *What's Going On*, *Hunky Dory* and *Led Zeppelin IV*. To be honest, I think he was just glad someone was in his shop on a Tuesday afternoon.

One of my most enjoyable album-buying escapades happened when I tracked down two LPs I'd been seeking out on vinyl for years, by one of my favourite songwriters, the (fairly) obscure American Bob Lind. The fact that I already had the songs on a CD released in 2007 was beside the point. I had searched record stores from New York to Berlin for his two albums from the Sixties, *Don't Be Concerned* and *Photographs Of Feeling*, but eventually found them not far from my home in London, in the downstairs vinyl section of Flashback Records.

My excitement was such that I let out a muffled scream of delight, and felt I had to tell the woman behind the counter why I had a big smile on my face when handing over the cash (nine pounds for both, bargain of the century). As I finished explaining my glee, she simply retorted, "They've been waiting here for you." I neglected to tell her that a couple of years previously I had performed a lecture about Bob Lind and his music in front of a live audience at comedian Josie Long's club night Lost Treasures Of The Black Heart, where writers and comedians are invited to speak about a subject they hold dear and believe is worthy of wider acclaim. I even gave out 20 Bob Lind starter packs, containing a Lind compilation I had made and put on to CD as well as an essay I'd written on him.

I would later, in 2013, go on to have lunch with Bob in London and conduct an interview with him for my website. It seemed the only other person who had interviewed him on that UK trip was Jarvis Cocker on his BBC 6Music show. I was happy to be in such a small yet privileged group.

Back to what the woman in the shop said though. It was a response that perfectly encapsulates the notion that an album can feel like a cherished friend. They are there for you, through the good and bad times and, if chosen wisely, will not let you down.

It's easy to romanticise about albums but, then again, surely music and romanticism go hand in hand? At least they do more than say, romanticism and the painting-and-decorating industry. I mention this, as one of my best friends has his own painting-and-decorating business. He doesn't tend to talk about matt emulsion much over a drink, but get him started on the merits of Beck's *Sea Change* and there's no stopping him. I have to agree with him that it's Beck's finest record.

The game changer for me was at the age of 13, when The Stone Roses released their debut. It was a case of being the right age for the right album at the right time. It is, of course, now rightly regarded as a classic but I knew it was something special from the off. I have yet to hear a better album and doubt I ever will.

The love I and countless others have for it is brilliantly captured by Shane Meadows in his documentary on the band, *Made Of Stone*. I actually got into an argument about it once when someone was claiming that they never did anything as good ever again and so weren't fit for such adulation. I merely reminded him of Joseph Heller's reply to the question once posed to him along the lines of, "Why have you never written anything else as good as *Catch–22*?" To which he retorted, "No-one else has either."

I still sit with friends, play albums and enthuse about them. If drink is involved, I am prone to the expression, "It's fucking amazing!" – just three words, one an expletive – but they sum it all up.

I have extolled the virtues of everything from Serge Gainsbourg's *L'Homme a Tete De Chou* and The Beta Band's *Hot Shots II*, to *Billie Holiday At Storyville* and *Tappa Zukie In Dub*. There are many, many more besides and I hope many more nights like those still to be had.

The conversations on such evenings have often turned into great debates, with matters deliberated over including how *Adventure* by Television never gets the credit it deserves because of always being in the shadow of *Marquee Moon*; the fact that Captain Beefheart's *Trout Mask Replica* is overrated while *Safe As Milk* is undervalued, and how, during a certain point in the

Eighties, Boris Becker could rightly have been labelled Ivan Lendl's bugbear. That last one has nothing to do with music but sometimes we stray off topic.

Incidentally, *Adventure* by Television is not only one of several albums I own on both CD and vinyl, but also one of my two greatest charity-shop finds. On the same day I uncovered the original Elektra vinyl, together with lyric sheet, I also came across Howlin' Wolf's *The Howlin' Wolf Album*, which features the man himself, backed with a full band doing psychedelic-esque rock versions of his songs.

The album is more famous for the fact that Wolf didn't like it, and this disdain is referenced on the cover, which reads: 'This is Howlin' Wolf's new album. He doesn't like it. He didn't like his electric guitar at first either.' It's actually very good indeed and worth the £10 that went straight to Oxfam. I still regret not buying The Fall album *Shift–Work*, which was also there that day – what a hat-trick that would have been. I made the classic charity-shop error of intending to go back the next day and get it, by which time, of course, it had already been snapped up.

I have also embraced download culture, especially the purchasing of single tracks. We probably all own albums we bought because we had heard a great tune from it, only to find out the rest of the album is a tad poor or, on other occasions, utter dross. It's also the case that downloads are cheaper than a physical copy, or free if illegality is factored in, not that I would endorse such activity, as musicians deserve to earn a living like the rest of us.

Also, it can be extremely difficult to find some songs

without going online. The only way I got my hands on 'In Zaire' by Johnny Wakelin, or Paul Davidson's reggae version of The Allman Brothers tune, 'Midnight Rider', was via iTunes. It was quick and easy, and saved a lot of hassle trying to track down obscure physical formats featuring a particular song.

There are some, however, that will only ever be found after a long hunt. I finally got my hands on the NF Porter track, 'Keep On Keeping On', from a bloke in Yorkshire, who was selling the compilation Northern Soul album, *The Golden Torch Story*, on which the track is contained.

Download culture has, of course, changed the way we listen to music, and I think it's a shame that listening to an album from start to finish is becoming increasingly less commonplace. There is much satisfaction to be had by playing an LP in its entirety, and the journey contained therein. I also like reading books from start to finish, as opposed to just chapter 7.

I've published several Albums Of The Year lists online over the years, as it's a chance to right some of the wrongs from the usual end-of-year polls, but also, and more importantly, an attempt to highlight some records that never got the attention they deserved. These have included Darker My Love's *Alive As You Are*, The Middle East's *I Want That You Are Always Happy* and The Warm Digits' *Keep Warm... With The Warm Digits*.

It's gratifying to introduce people to good music they haven't yet heard and for them to let you know they like it – a highly enjoyable public service, if you will. It's also an excuse, not that one should be needed, to listen to as much music as possible and, as a format for doing so, the album is incomparable.

7

THE CASTING PROCESS

I have quite a few friends who are professional actors and even the ones who are seemingly very successful are still going up for auditions, whether they be for television shows, plays or commercials. It would appear that, unless you are part of the Hollywood A-list, you still have to prove your worth, time and time again, via the audition process.

I have certainly enjoyed the acting jobs I have been involved in, ranging from independent short films to the Belle and Sebastian film, *Write About Love*. Mercifully, I didn't have to audition for those parts, thanks to the excellent taste and judgement of all involved.

However, the audition process has always intrigued me and when I was asked if I would like to attend a commercial casting, I thought it would, at the very least, be an interesting and valuable experience – regardless of the fact that to some, it seems, a dreadfully stressful process. I figured that it could pay to be seen by certain casting directors who also cast for films and television programmes.

I could see it all panning out, some high-powered player going: "Remember that Scottish guy who auditioned for the lager commercial? He had something about him, didn't he? I think he would be perfect for the six-part series being touted as a mixture of *Mad Men* and *The Sopranos,* with a hint of *Gregory's Girl*, which is going to be shown on the BBC in Britain and HBO in America." At the time of writing, I have yet to be offered this role but I did attend a few castings.

This is how, in my experience at least, a typical casting tends to pan out. I have chosen to regale in the present tense, as any good actor should always be in the moment:

I get a call the day before, saying there's an audition I'm deemed suitable for and am given an allotted time to turn up and do my thing. Sometimes you are given ample information as to what the advert is about, but other times details can be quite vague. On most occasions, there is a short script emailed through, along with a note saying, *Actors should be off–page for tomorrow's casting*, meaning the script should be committed to memory.

This always puts the fear into me. I hate learning lines. I think that's why I like to ad-lib as much as I can in whatever work environment I find myself. Of course, it's all very well ad-libbing but if the powers-that-be want you to stick to a script, you have to stick to a script. For me, this normally involves reading over the thing many times, then doing the same out loud, whilst smoking one too many cigarettes.* I won't sleep well the night before, either.

The next day I arrive for the casting roughly 20 minutes early. I do this because I can't stand to be late for anything – it's one of my major plus points. I like to find the door where the audition is being held and then walk round the block a few times, until it's two minutes before I'm due, at which point I ring the buzzer.

I then go up a flight of stairs, as castings always seem to take place on the first floor. I proceed to give my name to whoever greets me (usually a woman) and inform them that I'm there for the audition. I'm then given a sheet to fill out, with spaces for my name, agent details, clothing sizes and whether or not I have a valid passport and driving licence.

Normally I am also given a copy of the script to look over, along with the other actors who are up for the audition, often recognisable ones from film and television, who are sitting quietly and avoiding looking at each other.

It's at this point I take my seat and join in the eye-contact avoidance game. I can't help but feel everyone is thinking the same thing, something along the lines of, 'Hey, fuck you. I should be getting this gig and not you.' That's the impression I get anyway.

At some point, my name is called and I walk into a room where there could be one to five people ready to watch the audition. There is almost always a casting director present, sometimes the director and a cameraman to film you trying to impress those that matter.

Before I start the audition, I'm asked to give my name, the name of my agent and to show my hands to camera. The first time I was asked to do this, it took me by surprise but, mercifully, I always keep my fingernails clean. It would also appear to be the case that if you have less than two functioning and reasonably attractive hands, a career in commercial advertising may be an ill-advised route to take.

It's then time to audition. You may be asked to do it a few times, in fact. You then thank them for seeing you and leave the room, after which you walk past the other actors, still waiting to go in and still avoiding eye contact with each other. You then descend the inevitable flight of stairs before getting back out to the pavement. At this point, you light up a cigarette, take a long draw and think to yourself, 'Well, I totally fucked that up', or, if it's gone well, 'Christ, I'm glad that's over, hmm... I think I'm in with a chance there.'

That, in general, are how things play out, but each casting differs from another, ranging from the relatively straightforward to the bizarre and ridiculous. An actor can but rely on their skills or, failing that, luck.

A Kindle in New York City

The chance to film in New York is always enticing and, when the opportunity to fly there for a few days and film a 30-second advert for Amazon's Kindle devices was up for grabs, I was understandably keen. To be more specific, the role was for a warm, friendly and articulate man, between 30 and 35 years, and who also happens to be obsessed with his new Kindle. The script was short and featured two characters, the man and his wife. I assumed the lines for the wife would be voiced by the director, as had been my experience at previous auditions.

I received notification of this one on the way back from Brighton, where I'd been shooting a short film. No bother though, it was a short script and it would just be me, the director and a camera (which the director would also operate).

By way of preparation, I was sent an earlier American version of the advert which featured a guy and a girl. Basically, the guy had a Kindle and the girl didn't. The premise was that she is stressed out about getting to a bookshop in time to buy a new novel, while he simply downloads it in under 60 seconds, thus demonstrating the advantages of the product.

The next day, I made my way to Clerkenwell, where the studio was based, and waited in the rain for 20 minutes before pressing the buzzer. I walked up a flight of stairs and was greeted by a woman whom I presumed must be a casting director, and who asked me to take a seat and fill out the information form. It was when the casting director asked if I was going to do the scene with her that alarm bells began to ring. I was, in fact, about to audition with an actress who would be playing my wife.

This was worrying, as I had no idea I would be auditioning with a live actress. Consequently, I was convinced she would notice very quickly that I had no professional training and feel that it's a disgrace for someone like her (who had, no doubt, trained at acting school and been in all manner of touring plays while waiting on her big break) to have to do a scene with a novice.

I came to the conclusion that I would have to 'act' at being an actor before we even started acting out the scene. This manifested itself by me doing my utmost to show no visible sign of nerves and, in my head at least, making up anecdotes from my time spent at The Central School Of Speech & Drama, where I was viewed as both talented and sociable.

The one saving grace is that the part I was playing required me to be engrossed in my Kindle, while not paying too much attention to my wife who was determined to get to the bookshop.

We went for it and I have to say that I was impressed by the way she immediately became the character, like a switch had been turned on. She was suddenly playing the part of a busy wife. I wasn't married and so couldn't rely on previous experience. Luckily, I had been slightly disinterested in certain relationships in the past and decided to rely on that for inspiration instead.

It seemed to work to an extent, as the director said we had good chemistry. This visibly pleased the actress more than it did me, as I had a feeling everyone auditioning that day would be told they have good chemistry too, in an effort to elicit more confidence in them for the scene.

I may be wrong, of course, but I've heard my fair share of industry bollocks over the years and so now I take everything with a pinch of salt. I did nod in appreciation though, as if to say, "Well, thank you for that. As trained actors, we were hoping for chemistry."

We ended up doing the scene three times, with the director giving the actress some direction but none to me. I couldn't figure out if this was because I was simply doing a great job, or that the director already viewed me as a lost cause and any extra direction was superfluous. On the third and final take, I forgot my last line but we completed the scene regardless. This forgetfulness still rankled with me after I'd thanked the director, done the same to my on-screen wife, walked down the flight of stairs, opened the door back on to the pavement and lit a cigarette while believing that, although I hadn't quite messed it up, I hadn't nailed it either. As it happened, there would be no callback but, with it, no great surprise.

La Nouvelle Vague with Beer Accompaniment

This casting was for Stella Artois, and there was a fair bit to go on. I was up for the part of 'Paul', a barman attending a class with other barmen, in order to be taught how to pour the perfect pint by the beautiful 'Audrey', who is taking the class.

I liked the sound of Paul. He was unconventionally attractive, enigmatic, charming and likeable – this I knew from the character description. He was the perfect French New Wave man but not a chiselled model. He was meant to be cool, without trying to be. Of prime importance was the actor's ability to be able to handle subtle humour well.

It was also mentioned that Paul was the one who would interact with Audrey the most. There was no indication as to the shooting location, but one could only hope it was at most a short bus ride from the 6th arrondissement.

I was eager to bag the role. The Stella Artois

commercials I had seen in recent years recalled the French New Wave of cinema and they said that this new advert would be akin to a Jean-Luc Godard movie. Given that I'll never be in one of his films, this was definitely the next best thing. I really wanted it.

There was also going to be a very pretty girl in the advert and that could only be viewed as a bonus. We would probably get on well, start dating, end up getting married, and laugh about how we met on a Stella Artois commercial. This would be some time in the future, of course, and so I would first have to concentrate on the audition. There were only a few lines and I imagined there would be one person behind a camera voicing the lines of Audrey.

I was feeling very good about the situation, as I made my way to the studio just off Leicester Square. My state of quiet self-confidence was immediately rocked on arrival though. There were male models everywhere. Loads of the bastards, all with stupid haircuts and t-shirts with plunging necklines. This was not the Godard way. If you are going to wear a t-shirt to such a casting, at least make it a blue-and-white striped one that looks vaguely French, of the kind Brian Jones wore in 1965.

This only served to unsettle and anger me in equal measure. The outline document specifically stated that they were looking for men who weren't chiselled models or had conventional good looks. These guys were straight out of Milan, or wherever else male models hang out – and I wager had no appreciation of the Nouvelle Vague or were able to drink four pints of Stella without turning into a blabbering wreck. I could drink a keg of Stella and still extol the virtues of Godard, Truffaut and Rivette without slurring. I'd give it a good shot anyway and still be fit enough to read a chapter of Sartre's *Nausea* before feeling like puking myself.

This self-righteousness was quickly curbed when I realised there were, in fact, two castings going on at the same time: one for Stella, and one for a new VO5 hair product, hence the male models. It was only then that I clocked two unconventional, yet not wholly unattractive, blokes sitting quietly in the corner with their scripts. These were my competitors.

When I was called, it was surprising just how many people were in the room. I counted seven but tried not to let my eyes dart about too much, as I had to remain focused. I was introduced to the director and some other people, but it still wasn't clear what their roles were.

The director was American and appeared confident, self-assured and, in my view at least, a bit of an arse. He may well have been a nice chap but the way he sat with one foot on a table, acting all nonchalant, didn't sit well with me. I felt decidedly prickly. There I was about to act out a scene for his benefit, while bearing my artistic soul, and he couldn't even be bothered to take his foot off the table. He deserved a foot up his arse, I surmised at the time.

I did the scene once, pretending to be Paul speaking to Audrey, and it didn't go too badly. I felt suitably attractive in an unconventional way, but with a sense of charm and underlying vulnerability. The woman behind the camera delivered the lines and I responded at all the correct points. On finishing the scene, I couldn't help but feel everyone in the room was thinking, 'Well, if he's not our Paul, I don't know who is!'

The director then piped up, "Ok, that was good, but could you do it again but a bit less smiley?" Less smiley? I knew I didn't look glum but I wasn't aware of how smiley I was. Rest assured, I could do 'less smiley', no problem. So, once again, I played out the scene with less of a smile and more of an enigmatic, 'willing to learn how to pour the perfect pint' whimsy to my facial gestures.

They must be loving this, I thought to myself – the director had even taken his foot off the table. This was to be the moment they were to find their Paul, and I would become a new Jean-Paul Belmondo figure for the internet-based, Stella Artois, Godard-aping commercial fanbase that was sure to rise up in approval of my work. I finished the scene, the director shuffled, sat up and said, "Ok, thank you very much." Nothing else. I was expecting a little more on the side of awestruck but I figured he had to remain cool about things. He was probably already bemoaning the fact that he had to sit through loads of other actors, while all the time knowing he had already found his Paul. We would probably even laugh one day about the fact that on first impressions I thought he was a bit of an arse.

I left the room, walked down a flight of stairs and out into the open air, where I felt I certainly hadn't mucked things up. After the smiley corrections, I put in a good performance, one which I felt merited a job offer. As it turned out, all my performance merited was telephonic silence, as no offer ever came. 'Bugger', I said to myself, 'I really wanted that.'

*(I have since given up both smoking and casting calls).

8

KNOWLEDGE, OPINION AND
NAME-DROPPING

To be a big name, with a proven track record and obvious skills, puts you in a strong position – ideal, really. If I were to pick just one of those three things to help with career advancement, however, I would be tempted to say to focus on being a big name, or at least try and raise your profile. In my experience, it really does seem to help, regardless of talent. This has always been the case to some extent, of course, but to see notoriety trump all other considerations, first hand, can still come as some surprise.

I knew I had reached something of a nadir when told directly that, although I fitted most of the criteria for a broadcasting job I was up for, there was just one snag. To be precise, I was told, "You tick every box, bar one: you're not famous enough." What made it worse was that I had no one to blame but myself. To quote King

Creosote from his 2005 album *Rocket D.I.Y.* – "what a klutz I was."

It could be viewed that, since beginning a career in broadcasting, I made the most catastrophic of errors in placing creativity and artistry ahead of celebrity. All that time wasted reading books, going to the cinema and gigs, writing essays and scripts, making short films, recording podcasts and countless other dead-end streets. Really, what was I thinking?

I would, from time to time, even talk to myself in the third person. "Oh, Douglas, why all these artsy-fartsy leanings and inclinations?" I would ask. That voice was nowhere to be heard, however, when, walking out of the cinema one afternoon, I received a phone call asking me to participate in a reality show where celebrities look for love with each other on a tropical island. Quite the query, especially when my mind was still on the movie *Factotum*, as it happens, the film adaptation of the Charles Bukowski book. I would decline the invitation, but would go on to buy the DVD of the film when it was released a few months later. It really is a great movie.

Staying on the purchase front, I once even bought a book of French poetry. Reading Baudelaire indeed, albeit with English translations. This was not in keeping with the times, as it seemed, on more than one occasion, that the only way left to appear on television was to dance and be judged, bake a cake and be judged or have a Twitter following perceived large enough to warrant a profile without any judging at all.

It was obvious that any form of poetry, French or otherwise, wasn't going to be a viable option for career advancement. At least Coleridge had opium to soften the blow.

***

Now obviously I've been a tad flippant in this chapter so far but a very real point to make is that it's an ever-changing landscape, not just in the media but seemingly in most industries. Just look at the music industry in recent years. It's had to completely re-invent itself. But when it comes to music broadcasting, I still feel that a vast insight is not just an advantage, but something of a must.

T–Story Love Song

As music is my foremost passion, it can be jarring to see or hear people presenting programmes about music when it appears their knowledge is somewhat lacking – or, worse still, if they are pretending to know much more than they do.

When it's throwaway pop, then fair enough, but for music deemed to have more substance, I believe knowledge should be an imperative. Like I always say, when I watch the news headlines, I like to think that the person reading them understands the stories as well. As I also like to say, you don't have to own a West Coast Pop Art Experimental Band album to qualify as a doyen of musicality, but it helps.

At times when I've been a music presenter, I've always tried to be honest and not pretend I liked everything. Even when I couldn't directly say I thought an artist was poor, I could deviate enough from the standard script in order to put across a different point of view. I recall once being handed a link at the T In The Park music festival I was presenting for the BBC, along the lines of: *and now, Ayrshire's finest – Biffy Clyro.* Now, whilst I have nothing against the band personally, they just don't cater to my tastes but they of course do for a great number of others. I did feel though that another musician was more deserving of the accolade and while I had no choice but to introduce the band, I made sure I changed the lines to the following: "To some, they are Ayrshire's finest. Others, of course, would say that title belonged to Belle and Sebastian's Stuart Murdoch." I'm not sure if anyone really cared too much, but I did and most probably any B&S fans watching did too.

The same weekend, I also made my feelings known on Ian Brown who, due to sound problems, had decided to throw his monitors off the stage. What some saw as petulance, I simply viewed as the erratic behaviour of a bona fide musical legend who co-wrote one of the greatest albums of all time. As I said on camera at the time, "If you have co-written as many classics as he has, then such behaviour is excusable – he's the only legend here."

Immediately after we had wrapped, the director told me Mr Brown was here to see me. I turned around and there he was. He had come to shake my hand and thank me. This was a moment. If the 13-year-old me had been told that one day such a meeting was going to take place, it would have seemed completely unbelievable. As it was, all I could think of at the time was the fact he smelt strongly of smoke, and all I could do was shake his hand and thank him for the music he created. He did have an impressive aura about him though, as well as a ready supply of weed (quite probably).

Due to the fact that music is so important to me, I always thought it equally important to be honest about my feelings to viewers and listeners. Two further examples again involve artists from Manchester...

Don't Watch Back in Anger

The first was when I was asked to contribute to a TV documentary on Oasis. When asked what I thought about their worldwide hit, 'Wonderwall', I was simply truthful and said it never did much for me and that if a top ten list of the band's songs were to be compiled, it didn't deserve to be in there. When the show was broadcast, there was a stream of people salivating over the apparent brilliance of the song and then me saying what I did. Sod it, I thought. At least I stuck to my guns. Fast forward to the Glastonbury Festival, where I was presenting BBC coverage and Oasis were the Friday headliners.

This is actually further proof of the bizarre aspects and ramifications of broadcasting. If you contribute to a documentary, you don't necessarily think you will bump into its subjects, or that the subjects had watched the documentary and had remembered what you had said in it about them. This is exactly what happened.

First up on the Friday was Noel Gallagher, who simply said to me whilst he was hanging around in the BBC hospitality area, "I watched you on that show, *10 Ways Oasis Changed The World*... I liked what you said." I immediately recalled what I had said and remembered it being reasonable and truthful, at least in my head. I did think he might have had better things to do with his time than watch documentaries on his band but maybe that's what multimillionaire musicians like to do, watch themselves and others talking about their music.

The next day, I would encounter his brother, Liam, who called me over to the Oasis tour bus and on approach asked, "You're Dougie, aren't you?" I replied with a simple "yes", all the time wondering if he too had seen the show but conversely believed 'Wonderwall' to be the greatest thing he was ever involved in. He reached out his hand to shake mine, saying, "I like you, man. You know the score." We proceeded to have a brief chat, after which I continued on my way, slightly confused as to what I could surmise from both encounters.

If there was a lesson in all of this, it was that it pays to say what you believe, not what you think you're supposed to. Furthermore, no matter how many singles sold or hits clocked up on YouTube, what millions of people feel to be one of the greatest songs of all time is a sentiment not altogether shared by those who wrote and recorded it.

The Appreciation Of Morrissey

The other Mancunian I saw that weekend – but sadly didn't speak to – was Morrissey. His set, a glorious mixture of solo and Smiths material, was my festival highlight, especially due to the fact that up until then I had never seen him live. On the last night of transmission, I, along with some other presenters, were discussing live on air our stand-out moments of the festival and I enthused about the Morrissey set. Sadly, this was met with derision from some who didn't share my opinion, but were quick to mention the other bands I didn't rate as their highlights.

I would later find out that Mark Radcliffe also chose Morrissey as his highlight so, for me, I was in good company. I have always respected him as a broadcaster ever since I listened to *Hit The North* on the old Radio 5, a show syndicated throughout the UK late at night when I was in my early teens.

That weekend was also notable for the fact that I got my mate Nigel a backstage pass and also room in my lodgings off-site, so he could dry off and wash on a daily basis. The sight of Nigel wilfully drinking beer supposedly for the presenting team and going about his business, unconcerned of the media hubbub, was a welcome one. He would casually, if a tad drunkenly, ask BBC radio DJs for directions to certain stages or of my whereabouts, as if they too were on a 'drink all you can' jolly – it was a 'never the twain shall meet' moment and superb to witness. He did drink a hell of a lot of free booze though. In his defence however, I know that at the time he had an up-to-date TV licence, so was as deserving as the other millions who had paid it, but just happened to be in a place where he could capitalise on the fringe benefits.

Fighting the Good Fight

As I have a love for many musical acts sadly not recognised by the masses, I even started playing a game on BBC 5Live's *Fighting Talk* where I would try and drop in as many band names as possible without it sounding too contrived. Just the thought of some of these groups being mentioned on national radio was tantalising, to say the least (even though it was on a station that was about news and sports, not music).

I remember in particular, on a question dealing with

German football, I managed to mention not just the obvious Kraftwerk, but also Neu! and Tangerine Dream. Other artists and songs I've mentioned include Count Five's 'Psychotic Reaction', the recorded output of Silver Apples, latest releases by Allah-Las and a whole lot more in between.

It is quite possible that, at most, only a small handful of listeners may have heard of these artists, let alone know any of their recorded output. This is no problem. The fact that they are just being named and put out there is a buzz for me, because they do not usually receive the recognition they deserve on such a public platform.

I was once talking to Stewart Henderson on the subject. Stewart is head of Chemikal Underground Records and organiser of the Scottish Album Of The Year Awards, as well as a big *Fighting Talk* fan. He told me that if just one person listening was to get an esoteric reference, musical or otherwise, then it's a result – and I believe that to be the case. This was at the forefront of my mind when I expanded my repertoire and started to name–drop classic works by novelists and poets as well as artistic movements, including Saul Bellow's *Dangling Man*, Coleridge's *Kubla Khan* and Dadaism. Wherever that one person who caught those references is, I'm glad they are out there.

The Household Name Game

Of course, one person out there picking up on obscure musical and literary references doesn't exactly help in making someone a household name and it brings me back to a salient point. As I have already stated, I have never been very interested in playing a celebrity game as, if you are not proper A-list, it can look rather pathetic. It seems it does help though. There is no doubting that a raised profile leads to more offers of work but it's unfortunate that other factors, such as knowledge, passion and skill, are sometimes apparently deemed of lesser importance.

If it is a case of doing seemingly anything to raise your profile, then I simply could not and cannot do it. However, not all have the same outlook. I've seen people making imbeciles of themselves on TV, doing all manner of things like running into snow naked, revealing intimate details about their marriage and generally acting like clowns at the bequest of some host or other.

You wonder how these people must feel when they are home alone, or what their families think when they see such behaviour. "Why did you do THAT on national television, Son?" "Because the producer, Xander, said it was a good idea, Dad." The thing is, perhaps two months or a year later, these same people will end up with their own show or a whole host of offers. It's some business I tell you.

Two Hours In London

Whilst it was always the intention to hit London with a bang on moving there it was not on my agenda to be put in the back of an ambulance and hospitalised within the first two hours.

The Director's Chair

While directing short films can involve no budget
whatsoever, thankfully one can at least find a chair to
sit on at times.

After The Evans

I always think that if you're going to someone's house to stay over, you should take them a gift regardless if they are on the breadline or multi-millionaires, in the case of Chris Evans it was the *After The Fox* soundtrack on heavyweight vinyl.

James Brown

Meeting bonafide musical legends like James Brown is tremendously exciting, meeting musical legends who sit down for a television interview with their new wife you have no background knowledge of and have no questions for is a bit odd.

Record Shopping

One of life's great pleasures is to spend time, sometimes several hours, in record shops in the hope you're about to stumble upon something special and then have the opportunity to play this music while DJ'ing at a club or gig night regardless if the people there have never heard certain songs before or indeed in some cases, ever again.

Fighting Talk

Appearing as a regular on BBC 5Live's *Fighting Talk* has been hugely enjoyable and while talking in humorous and informative terms about the latest sporting issues is an imperative on the show, it happily doesn't preclude the dropping into conversation of various musical, filmic and literary references as well.

The London Nobody Knows Now

In *The London Nobody Knows Now* I was determined to make a film looking at how the locations featured in the original 1967 film *The London Nobody Knows* had changed over time whilst critiquing the original film along the way. For it to be screened at the BFI to sell out audiences was a bonus and I hope James Mason would have approved.

Belle and Sebastian

In the Belle and Sebastian film *Write About Love* I played the dual roles of host and band manager which was twice as many as Robert De Niro in *Taxi Driver* but admittedly still six less than Alec Guinness in *Kind Hearts And Coronets*. Only one of us hasn't won an Academy Award.

Steven Spielberg

It's one thing having a conversation with Steven Spielberg, it's another entirely having a conversation with Steven Spielberg about his direction of the superb *Columbo* episode *Murder By The Book*.

Cathedrals For The Masses

Cathedrals For The Masses – a journey into the world of the football stadium. A show yet to be made but surely the world of the football stadium deserves to be documented and celebrated. It could even run to multiple series, a returning format no less but with added floodlight pylons.

9

TECHNOLOGY, FILMING, RECORDING AND CLUBBING

The role of technology to aid filming and recording – or to be more precise, recent advances in technology – cannot be underestimated. It led to three projects in 2014 that, just a few years previously, would have been almost impossible due to costs.

The first was my music podcast, *The Public Service Broadcast*. The idea behind it was to make the kind of radio show that I would not just like to present, but would also like to listen to. A nice cross-section of music, both new and old, with the addition of soundtracks and even spoken word. The public-service angle came from the fact that I felt I could let people hear great music previously unknown to them, but I also liked the old-fashioned BBC remit connotations.

I even went as far as having Miles record idents for it in his best old-fashioned BBC announcer's voice. The whole thing worked well and I didn't even need a studio.

Firstly, I compiled the music for each show and wrote the script. I then recorded the links in my spare bedroom, using a microphone my sound-recordist pal Stevie lent to me, straight onto my laptop. It was paramount during this process that all hard surfaces were covered with blankets, and the curtains drawn to get the best studio sound possible. Most importantly, I had to ensure that the toilet extractor fan wasn't on, as it made a hell of a noise through the adjoining wall. I'm sure Bob Dylan overcame similar problems when recording *Theme Time Radio Hour*.

After recording, I then placed the links and idents in between the tracks I was playing on a particular show (as it felt like a radio show more than just a podcast), using GarageBand on my laptop. After that, I would convert it all to an mp3 and upload it to Mixcloud for the world to listen to. This was DIY production with professional-sounding results. It was as liberating as it was exhilarating and I'm pleased to say people seemed to really enjoy them – whether it be strangers who got in touch to tell me so or established DJs I respect, such as BBC 6Music's Gideon Coe. I happily took the praise but neglected to tell them about my toilet-fan anxiety.

I was bang into audio recording in my new home studio and so, at the same time, set about producing my first audio book, *What To Talk About When There's Nothing To Talk About*. This was based on the weekly blog series I had written, which detailed some of the more exasperating and downright stupid things I would encounter on a day-to-day basis but which I felt were worthy of discussion. They included the sight of women still with scuffed price stickers on the soles of their shoes, the fear and confusion caused when two men's bare feet touch unexpectedly and some people's insistence on bastardising the word football for the flimsy 'footy'. I hoped that a blog series then audio book, free to download via SoundCloud, might even facilitate fresh discourse on the subjects. Whatever the case, it was just great to have the means to record and share such a thing with a wider audience.

Technology has also helped with filming, especially outdoors and, in particular, on the streets of London. Obviously, vast improvements to cameraphone technology have meant that it is entirely possible to make short films using the same device you text and make calls with. Honourable mention must go to the widely available Canon 5D camera though, which has proved something of a godsend, as it records high-quality digital film as well as still photographs. The fact that it looks like a still camera is a huge advantage, as it's obviously less intrusive in size and doesn't attract the attention of onlookers or the swathe of security guards in central London who seem intent on telling anyone filming that they are not permitted to do so. When I decided to make *The London Nobody Knows Now*, I knew that such a camera would be extremely beneficial.

Written by Geoffrey Fletcher and first published in 1962, *The London Nobody Knows* is a book that celebrates the lesser-known places and buildings of the metropolis. It's a good read, but even more intriguing to me was the film of the same name, made in 1967, and presented by none other than James Mason. It's a fascinating document of the city at the time and breathtaking to see how some places have changed – often completely – such as Spitalfields Market. The presenting technique of James Mason is also a delight to behold, with him managing to combine insight, dogmatism and humour throughout. The whole thing is a tad idiosyncratic, yet brilliant.

Ideally, I wanted to make an hour-length documentary on the film by visiting the same locations as Mason, spliced with the original footage in order to compare and contrast. It was the closest I would ever have to a time machine. It was also my intention to interview historians, documentary film-makers and fans of the film. This would be a huge undertaking as an independent project, so I opted to film a ten-minute taster that would see me talking about the film in the locations of the original. This I did whilst wearing the same kind of outfit that Mason wore in the original: notably a flat cap, jacket, trousers, shirt, jumper, a good pair of brogues and all the while carrying a classy looking umbrella.

My pleasure in the clothing worn was matched with the equipment used. What a joy that camera was. Along with my friend Ewan who owned the camera, we would jump on the tube or a bus with ease, as opposed to carting a quality, yet cumbersome, DVCPro HD camera. We also went practically unnoticed, which sped things up nicely. Admittedly, we did have a soundman with us but with radio mics it was very simple.

The hassles of the editing process were also alleviated due to technology. Whereas just a few years before, I would have tried to bag some out-of-office hours time on a studio Avid suite, I was now able to use Avid, along with a great editor who was a fan of the project, on an Apple computer in a house. A house of all things. As Russell Crowe's character, Captain Jack Aubrey, says in *Master and Commander: The Far Side Of The World,*

"What a fascinating and modern world we live in." The film is set in 1805.

On completion, a friend who works for the BFI saw it and suggested I submit it for the 2015 London on Film Festival at the BFI Southbank. Brilliantly, it was accepted on the condition that I could clear the rights for the original film, as I used about three minutes of it in mine. There was also a seven-second clip from Bob Dylan's 'Subterranean Homesick Blues' in there too, as it was filmed on the Savoy Steps, just along from where a scene from *The London Nobody Knows* was filmed. I thought this was worth drawing attention to in my film, especially as most people assume the video was shot in New York.

So, with regard to original *The London Nobody Knows* footage, I went to StudioCanal and was just plain honest with them. I told them I had made the film, used three minutes of their footage, did not do so for monetary gain and that I was seeking permission for it to be screened at the festival. They came back with quite the shocker – £400 per minute of footage used. This equated to £1200. It seemed to defeat the purpose of making the film in the first place, as everyone involved had provided their services for free because they believed in the project and wanted to see it made.

I went back to StudioCanal and told them all this, as I thought that if I was honest and they could see that it was purely someone with artistic intentions, well, they might take pity. It worked and they did. I was offered a deal whereby if I paid £150 to StudioCanal, I would secure the original rights to be shown at the BFI as part of *The London Nobody Knows Now*. What a great outcome and a hell of a saving – £1050. I was extremely thankful.

There still remained, however, the Bob Dylan footage clearance to be resolved. Due to the 'Subterranean Homesick Blues' video being part of the great DA Pennebaker documentary, *Dont Look Back* (he didn't use an apostrophe in the title for some reason), I knew that I would have to get in touch with Pennebaker Hegedus Films in New York. As one of the most iconic music clips of all time, my hopes weren't too high, as I assumed they must get inundated with requests to use the footage. And why would they agree to give some of it, albeit only seven seconds, to someone and something they had never heard of?

Regardless, I sent an email detailing what I had done. There was no reply. About a week later, I cut and pasted the exact same email and sent it once more. To my surprise, this did get a reply from DA's son, Frazer Pennebaker. So began a succession of emails back and forth across the Atlantic. He asked to see my film, liked it and suggested we 'barter'.

Now, I didn't have much to barter with but for a while it seemed a deal would be struck. We spoke about the possibility of me again filming the alleyway where his father had filmed, some 50 years previously. Such footage would be beneficial, as it seemed there was going to be a re-release of the film, and my footage would make for an interesting contrast with how the location looked half a century previously (remarkably similar as it happens).

The deal would be that I would simply send it to him and, in return, I would secure the seven seconds of footage rights from *Dont Look Back*, whilst crediting the original in my closing credits. Simple. Only it wasn't. For whatever reason, the lines of communication were snapped and I stopped getting replies to my emails. I kept sending them, but nothing returned. I suppose this kind of thing happens a lot, but it was strange that he appeared keen to sort out a mutually beneficial deal only to cease contact. It was a bugger, but at least I could still show myself walking through the alley and refer to *Dont Look Back* in the script, regardless of not securing the footage. Not ideal, but certainly not a disaster.

The London Nobody Knows Now would go on to be shown twice at the British Film Institute during the London on Film Festival, along with the original *The London Nobody Knows*. As a prelude to this, I was interviewed by the BFI about my film, and the online piece (also to be given out in a printed version at the screenings) went on to become one of the most shared interviews ever on the BFI website.

The screenings themselves were completely sold out and it felt like a hell of a personal creative achievement. I was also asked to introduce the film and took part in a Q&A after the second screening, which saw me answer questions posed by Head Curator for the BFI National Film Archive Robin Baker on how I went about making my own film and also my views on the original. The discussion was then opened out to the audience who seemed to enjoy the chat as much as I did.

I also made some BFI history, as it was the first time that a short had been screened after the main feature – as obviously it made sense to do so, helping as it did in contrasting London, then and now. I was also informed that it was the first time a director of a short-length film had been asked to take part in a Q&A. And so, for at least one week in July, I felt quite the trailblazer and could only hope James Mason, director of *The London Nobody Knows* Norman Cohen and writer of the book Geoffrey Fletcher would have approved.

Furthermore, I was asked if I would be willing to donate my film to the BFI archives. I saw this as an honour and also the chance of a legacy for my independent short-film work. That certainly made all those days making art for art's sake seem worth it.

DJing

Although using other people's material, I've always seen DJing as an artistic expression of sorts and definitely a way of getting good music out there. I have put on many club nights in London specialising in the music I love the most, with certain occasions springing to mind for different reasons. I will always be proud that I raised a couple of thousand pounds for Marie Curie Cancer Care by cycling from London to Paris in 2014. One of the ways I generated the sponsorship was putting on a night at the Betsey Trotwood pub in Farringdon and charging everyone a tenner to get in. That's the great thing about charity nights, you can up the entrance price and play on people's consciences, as it's all for a great cause.

I knew that, although the entrance fee was steeper than usual, those in attendance would hear the best music in London that Saturday night. A nice mixture of the finest indie, rock and roll, soul and obscure soundtrack music. It was at that night that somebody came up to me and asked somewhat sheepishly, yet eagerly, if I had just played a variation of the main theme from *Zulu*. I had done just that. It's a Sixties beat version of the main theme called 'Monkey Feathers' and can be found on the b-side of the official soundtrack, the original vinyl of which I was playing that night.

Interestingly, the reason that song and the others on the b-side exist is because when the original soundtrack had been recorded by John Barry, it quickly became evident that it all fitted onto one half of a record, with the other side needing filling up. Quickly, a series of beat versions were made and even an official dance, 'Zulu Stamp', commissioned. Not only that but the choreographer was none other than Lionel Blair, long before he was a team captain on *Give Us A Clue* and a participant in the chair-swapping hilarity that ensued therein.

Back to DJing though. Another evening that sticks in the mind was a club called Dirty Little Secret, which a pal of mine was putting on at Madame Jojo's in Soho. Three bands would play, with each being accompanied by a different burlesque dancer, and I would play songs before, during the breaks in bands and afterwards. Well, those dancers could certainly dance and they looked amazing, as I told them when I was chatting to them backstage. The fact that they would often be in states of partial undress at the time can only be seen as a perk of the job.

Things would get more fruity front of house, however. When one band were on, I went upstairs to get some air and sat with Justine – whose club it was and who was working the door. I took up position and helped her stamp people on the hand as they came in and gave their money. It was when one female was paying her money that I got quite the fright as, upon telling her I needed to give her a stamp, she retorted, "stamp this", and presented her ample left breast. I duly stamped it and I believe she went on to have an enjoyable night – as did I in no small part due to my front-of-house activities.

Djing isn't all about tits, though. I've always enjoyed playing at gigs more than club nights. The reason is that when bands are the main part of the night, you don't necessarily have to play tunes for people to dance to, just music to keep a good vibe in the room. You can play more experimental stuff if you fancy, as long as it's in keeping with the mood. I've played all sorts of things at gigs but, as long as you don't alienate the room, you're OK.

I get so tired of those indie nights when you're just waiting on 'Blue Monday' by New Order or 'Take Me Out' by Franz Ferdinand to come on, as the DJ has to play it to ensure people dance to very well known tunes. I understand why though, especially at the weekend. If you're putting on an indie-orientated club and people want to dance, you'll always have a pretty big contingent that are drunk and want to listen to things they have heard a thousand times before. Don't get me wrong, they are great tunes but they're played to death. I remember once playing The Smiths classic b-side, 'You Just Haven't Earned It Yet Baby', at a club, only for a drunken punter to come up and demand 'Panic' was played instead. I couldn't be doing with that and, as a result, could never put on a club to attract punters solely to make money, even under the guise of 'alternative' or 'indie' music.

Ideally, I would love to have an avant-garde indie night

where I could play my favourite guitar-orientated songs, but also soul, electronica and even stuff that you can't hear anywhere else when you go out, such as the aforementioned *Zulu* b-sides or the majestically funky 'Les F...' by everyone's favourite Belgian, Jacques Brel, taken from his final studio album from 1977, *Les Marquises*. The evening would be complemented with standing lamps, candles, a bar you could get served at by attentive staff, seats and tables and, of course, girls wanting to get their boobs stamped. It's my club version of George Orwell's *The Moon Under The Water* and, like him, I'd also be in favour of a snack counter where mussels are the speciality of the house.

10

CASTING CALLS: THE FINAL ACT

There were several more castings I would attend with various degrees of success – a few callbacks, shortlisted for some and ignored for others. I even at one stage found myself filming a short sequence in my own living room as requested by Jonathan Glazer who was casting for his latest film *Under The Skin* starring none other than Scarlett Johansson. Alas, I didn't bag the role but at least the director of Sexy Beast and music videos for Radiohead, Blur and Massive Attack got to see what colour my sofa was.

When I told some full-time actors I know that I had received callbacks and made shortlists, they seemed very impressed, as they had yet to receive any after four years' training at recognised drama schools. After some consideration, I thought it unwise to suggest them taking a post graduate course in the meantime until their luck changed, especially when factoring in the tuition fees.

Although at times I felt way out of my comfort zone when attending auditions, there were others who seemed to be having nervous breakdowns at the sight of a script and casting director. One particular downfall happened in Glasgow, where I had flown in order to bag an American advert that would feature, of all things, a Scottish gardener. The money on offer – something in the region of £20k – was obviously amazing, but so was the thought of filming in LA.

Sadly, it wasn't to be. I would eventually lose out to actor Phil McKee, who was in *Band of Brothers*, one of my all-time favourite television series. No disgrace in that, but it would have been less of a blow to lose out to *Band of Brothers* main man Damian Lewis, especially on the back of his *Homeland* success.

Anyway, as I waited my turn to go in, I could hear everything that was going on, as there was only a thin door between the actors waiting and the one currently auditioning. What I heard as I waited my turn was a person who couldn't even say the words, let alone act them. Stumble, stop. Stumble, stop. A complete attack of nerves, perhaps?

I then heard the casting director ask the actor if he would like to step out for a couple of moments and then come back in and try again. This was awful. He now had to come out and face those waiting – three of us by this point – all having heard his meltdown. It was cruel but I could guess what everyone waiting to go in was thinking: 'Thank fuck this isn't happening to me! Please let me go in next, as this is the best support act I could have wished for.'

After composing himself for a few moments, the chap

(who could only have been in his early 20s) went back in. It started all over again. Stumble, stop. Stumble, stop. It was harrowing to sit through and, when we all heard the casting director saying she thought they should leave it there, it came as a relief to everyone concerned. I then went in, nailed it, got the plane back to London and waited on the call, along with my flight and accommodation details for LA. Still waiting as it happens.

Perhaps the one saving grace for the chap in Glasgow was that at least he could speak English, which couldn't be said for another actor whom I did an audition with for a car manufacturer. The premise of the scene was that my character was a very picky potential car buyer with many requirements, but was unaware that the person he was speaking to was merely a mechanic and not a salesman.

This was all fine in theory, but it transpired my co-anchor was Russian and could barely understand, let alone speak, English. I still don't know how he got the audition in the first place. This didn't stop him deciding to take his vest off during the second take, as he seemed to think that mechanics should operate with less clothes than other tradesmen. Perhaps that's what they do in Omsk? I've no idea, never been there.

The fact that he performed this striptease spontaneously during a take surprised me greatly, and reminded me of the scene in *Twins*, when Danny DeVito believes Arnold Schwarzenegger has a disease, due to his huge muscles appearing to be an unfortunate swelling. I was ready for him to launch into 'Yakety Yak' at any given moment.

Although I had to admire his improvisational efforts, he displayed absolutely no reactions to my actions, even though responsiveness is one of the key elements of good acting – or so I have read. He really didn't seem to know what was going on and, as a result, I found myself delivering lines about cars to a man who was naked from the waist up and seemingly disinterested and confused at everything I was saying. I would go on to be shortlisted for the job but, alas, not offered the role in the end. Unsurprisingly, the Russian didn't get the job either but, in his defence, I too have found some castings bewildering, such as the one I did for Johnnie Walker whisky.

The storyline alone for this advert was enough to warrant it being written into a full-length graphic novel. In a nutshell, it was about a village that sits at the bottom of a curved valley. Through a chance encounter, one man realises that there is a wondrous place above them, on the other side of their world, one that they could never have imagined in their wildest dreams. He discovers a way to get out of their dark and unattractive surroundings, and encourages the whole village to walk en masse in a shared quest to discover the amazing place that he has glimpsed in the sky.

What this amazing place exactly was remained unclear, but it seemed you would have to be pissed up on whisky to come up with an idea like that in the first place. The specifications for the male actor were that he should have dark hair, an expressive face and a mysterious look in his eyes. He should also be rugged but not trampy, charismatic and be able to handle dialogue and non-verbal acting.

I was glad I hadn't shaved for a few days as, due to a

complete absence of muscles, my stubble would have to constitute all my ruggedness. I'll admit though, my hope wasn't strong that I would get the part. This definitely sounded like one for 'proper' actors, and by that I mean actors who have trained for at least a day.

So, I put this one down as a way of gaining valuable experience, which was just as well, as, if I had gone in there hoping to nail it, I would have been disappointed. There was a bit of workshopping involved, as I proceeded to pretend I had just found the most beautiful flower imaginable, that I was gazing into a dark sky, wondering if there was a better life to be had somewhere else and finally rounding up imaginary villagers to tell them about the amazing place I'd glimpsed amongst the clouds.

At one point I even beckoned a villager called Derek to come over. I've no idea where that name came from. I was as far out of my comfort zone as I had been at any of the castings I ever attended. It didn't feel necessarily bad; it just didn't feel particularly good either. All I could muster for certain was that I was again pretending to be an actor and doing what I thought an actor would do in that situation. There was no room for comedy either, something that would at least have made me feel more comfortable.

I can honestly say that, at that moment, I wasn't sure if what I was doing was satisfactory but not good enough to bag the job, or if it was just complete and utter shit. I was still unsure when I left the studio, but tried to counter this uncertainty with the fact that it's sometimes difficult to critique one's own acting and that there may well have been enough in my performance to warrant a callback. This was the positive spin I put on matters as I made my way home. Turns out I was wrong to spin so positively, as there was no callback ever to be had.

Thankfully, a more comedic opportunity was just around the corner and one where my improvisational genius would shine, due to a complete accident. I was playing the part of an undercover agent who, for some reason, a leading windscreen-repair company thought appropriate to interest a new demographic to their product. One of the points of reference given was that it should incorporate 'dry and subtle humour'.

I was also instructed to pretend to be in a car chase and then stop the vehicle in a dingy car park and confront some criminals with my gun. I was handed a plastic gun and away we went. As I got out my imaginary car and began to walk across an imaginary car park, all the while being watched by a casting director in a small room, I was concentrating so much on the subtleties of the performance that I dropped the gun. Thankfully, as I despairingly tried to pick it up as quickly as possible and continue across the car park, I noticed the casting director laughing and, on completion of the scene, she congratulated me on a great piece of improvisation.

Apparently, I was the only person who had dropped the gun for comedic effect and it worked very well indeed. I nodded my head in agreement – no need to tell her it was a complete accident.

So there you have it – concrete proof, if it were needed, that brilliance is sometimes ineptitude in disguise. Strange game, acting, strange game, indeed.

11

WORKING WITH ONE OF YOUR FAVOURITE BANDS

The chance to meet a favourite band is a very exciting proposition but to be asked personally to collaborate with them is another thing entirely. When Stuart Murdoch of Belle and Sebastian asked if I would work with the band, I was surprised, excited and hungover in equal measure.

The night before I had been having dinner at a friend's house, where a lot of red wine was consumed whilst listening to music. The very last song played that night was 'Lazy Line Painter Jane' by Belle and Sebastian, but little did I know how prescient that would be.

I made my way home, fell into bed and passed out. As I didn't have a very early start the next day, I planned on taking my time getting up but was awoken by my phone ringing around 9am. It was Stuart, who had got my number from his wife, whom I worked with when I hosted a series of live interviews with film-makers for BAFTA.

He told me that the previous day he had chaired a band meeting all about a film they wanted to make. It was to take the form of a television show and would act as a showcase for the band's forthcoming album, *Write About Love*. They weren't interested in the traditional promotional route of going around various radio stations and TV shows. Instead, they wanted to film something independently, which could be a stand-alone piece as well as a promotional tool. Furthermore, they wanted me to present it.

Stuart told me I was the first and last person on their list of who they wanted to front the film, which I obviously took as a great compliment – as I stood in my bedroom feeling like my head was being squashed in a vice, following the previous night's alcohol consumption. This didn't detract from the exhilaration of being asked to work with the band, however – and, as a result, a few minutes later I was dancing round the living room whilst exclaiming the traditional phrase, "Ya fucking dancer!" I was still in a state of partial undress as this happened.

Over the coming weeks, I would speak to Stuart several times and, although I kind of got what he was after, it was all still a bit vague. He didn't want me to present along the lines of, "With a song from their new album, here are Belle and Sebastian." This was fine by me, as generic presenting does my head in. Instead, he wanted it to be more left-field, more philosophical and, in his exact words, "more Tony Wilson".

We also discussed that, as the whole band would be

performing at least two new songs from the record, it would be a cost-effective way to get two new videos done – now that the old music-industry business model was completely shattered by the internet age.

As a date for filming, as well as my modest fee, were arranged, my excitement grew. To be honest, I would have done it for free but it was nice to receive payment for it. It got me thinking though. I was aware how privileged a position I was in as a fan of the band and didn't want to mess it up. If I did, how could I ever listen to them again? I'd probably have to burn all my B&S records to banish the memory, just as Simon Pegg's character, Tim, in *Spaced* destroys his *Star Wars* memorabilia due to *The Phantom Menace* tarnishing the reverence surrounding the original three films. I was also aware that they had asked me as fans of my work, so I didn't want to appear like a competition winner, however much it may have felt like it.

There was one very real niggling problem though. Even as I boarded my plane to fly to Glasgow, there was literally no script – nothing whatsoever. Now, I like to ad-lib as much as possible and completely stray off topic when the mood takes me, but to do so you have to have a topic to stray away from in the first place. With no script, what is the starting point, let alone what to ad-lib about? (This is something I would later go on to discuss with veteran music writers and broadcasters David Hepworth and Mark Ellen on *The Word* magazine podcast.)

That evening I had dinner with Stuart in the hope that finally there might be a script, not something to learn off by heart, but certainly something to work and deviate from. No chance – he just wanted me to make it up. This was fine in theory, but what if the stuff I made up was sub-standard? I didn't want to be the one who was going to let the whole thing down and, as a result, I had a very bad night's sleep. I woke early the next day and wrote some cod-philosophical babble that didn't sit particularly well either, but, over breakfast, I came up with material I thought was certainly good enough to use. It was a relief for sure.

When I got to location, I felt I needed to double-check with Stuart and the film's director, Blair Young, that what I had written was satisfactory. I was apprehensive but, thankfully, they thought it was just the right tone and exactly what the piece required.

It wasn't lost on me that I was getting to see one of my favourite bands (Belle and Sebastian have equal billing with The Smiths, The Rolling Stones and The Beta Band in my top bracket) close up and performing brand-new songs nobody had yet heard outwith the band themselves. I hadn't had an experience like this since watching The Beta Band soundcheck before recording a live set for *The Beat Room* (the TV show I presented for BBC2 Scotland before moving to London).

I wasn't alone though, as the band had invited a number of fans to be part of the audience who would watch them mime two new tracks, 'I Want The World To Stop' and 'I Didn't See It Coming'. To hear these songs for the first time was exhilarating, and they remain my album highlights.

Between takes, I would film my links, whilst cameras were being re–positioned, and chat to the band. I remember talking to guitarist Stevie Jackson about the great Neil Young song, 'Revolution Blues', as well as our mutual love of The Rolling Stones.

I would also go on to conduct a Q&A with the band and audience, and appear in shot watching the band mime the aforementioned tracks. I ended up recording three links, two of which I had written just a few hours before. Thankfully, as I had already consulted Stuart and Blair over them, I felt they had the right balance of what Stuart wanted and what I was all about as a performer. It's worth repeating that this was quite a tall order, as it was difficult not to 'talk in specifics but still make sense' in line with Stuart's wishes, while all the time doing something that I was happy to put my name to as well.

The opening link going into 'I Want The World to Stop' went as follows: "People sometimes think about what music can add, such as atmosphere at a party or a wedding – you may have been to either, or indeed both. It's the same with subdued lighting, given the correct candle or indeed lampshade choice. More importantly, is what music can give – excitement, gratification, empathy and comfort. So, with this general ethos in mind, let me not add but give to you, Belle and Sebastian."

I'm sure no one in the world has ever introduced a band like that or ever will do again. My cod-philosophy would, I hope, have made Tony Wilson proud, or at least met with his approval. My closing link took a similar tone, with the only direction given to me to end on a positive note, as the song was a positive one – again without doing the usual "and to close the show with such and such a song..." Here's what I said going into 'I Didn't See It Coming': "You fall over in the street, you get back up again. You run out of milk for your morning macchiato, you simply go to the shop and buy more. You go to a poster arcade to buy your favourite design, perhaps in A3, it's not open, you go back the next day... unless it's a bank holiday, in which case it's probably best to go back on the Tuesday or Wednesday. Point being, things normally work out the way they should and, more often than not, for the better. On that note, I give you Belle and Sebastian." I'm not sure where in my head the ideas of coffee and posters came from but, as I'd already spoken about lamps and candles, it didn't seem too out of place.

I did have one last trick up my sleeve that day. I had at the time just finished editing my short film *Timber!* and the script was still very much in my head. There was one scene I had decided to delete purely for time constraints, despite the fact it included dialogue I really liked. Not only that, the words seemed to fit perfectly with the whole ethos of the film we were now making, as they concerned music and love but were non-specific to Belle and Sebastian. I told the director I had an idea for another link that I thought was worth filming and recited it to him. He was very impressed with the following, apparently just thought up on the spot: "It's been claimed love is the answer. It's also been queried that if love is the answer, what is the question? And that's something which can be confusing, as the question could quite rightly be put as simply as, 'What is the key to everlasting happiness?' At the same time, though, the same answer would be derived from the following question: 'What Sixties band fronted by Arthur Lee released the seminal *Forever Changes* album in 1967?' Confusing times, indeed. I may need to take a seat..."

Of course, it had been written and filmed some six

months previously, but there was no need to tell anyone that, as I was happy to give the impression that my awe-inspiring brain was able to work in such a fashion. I genuinely thought it would work though, and thankfully it did. Soon after, we wrapped and retired to a pub but there was still work to be done the following day.

This time, there was character acting involved. After filming had finished on day one, Stuart informed me he had another idea he wanted to incorporate into the film, that of me playing the part of the band's manager.

This was now a 'dual-role production' and only two behind Peter Sellers in *Dr Strangelove*. Admittedly, still six behind Alec Guinness in *Kind Hearts And Coronets*, but double that of Robert De Niro in *Taxi Driver*, which I think speaks volumes.

The next morning, I was to make my way to a college in Glasgow where I would lecture the band on how the new album should be promoted. Not only that, but the words I uttered would be taken from a real email from the real manager of Belle and Sebastian, who had sent a long message out to all the band. This was now very much a multi-layered concept and I loved it.

It was bizarre to face the group, who were instructed to look as bored as possible while I lectured them on how the music industry had changed, and how they had to change with it. It was actually a pretty good lesson for any musician but I was mainly concentrating on my acting.

When we were all done on day two, I travelled through to Edinburgh for a few days to see family but would be back in Glasgow the next week for more acting, but this time without words.

That day's filming saw me walking around streets in Glasgow city centre, on the underground, on a multi-storey roof and in a park. I was to appear thoughtful and dejected over the band's apparent apathy and disinterest at being told about the present state of the music industry and their place in it. I really did enjoy all of this. I felt I was part of some kind of arthouse piece and it suited me down to the ground. I was eager to see the results and, only around a week later, a taster was released.

It came out, if I may use the technical parlance, cool as fuck. The band looked great, it was beautifully filmic and I was pleased with the way I appeared. This was certainly a different way for a band to promote a new album and, on the strength of the taster alone, it totally worked. Only a couple of weeks later and having returned to London, the whole show was edited and I was very pleased with what I saw, which was as much a relief than anything else. I hadn't messed it up and could listen to my B&S records in the future with a clear conscience.

Even the broadsheets seemed to get it, albeit with some factual inaccuracies. For example, *The Guardian* wrote about it favourably, although the running time was half an hour, not 20 minutes – and the Q&A concentrated solely on music. I must admit though that the description of the whole thing being 'slightly oddball' made me smile. The review read as follows: 'After a four-year break, Glasgow's foremost soul janglers are returning with a new album, *Write About Love*, next month. Never averse to doing things differently (in a few weeks they play a cemetery gig), their website now hosts their own 20-minute TV show, which features the band playing live, taking part in an audience debate and acting in deadpan sketches about the state of the music biz; comedian Dougie Anderson stars as the host and the band's stressed-out manager. It's brilliantly filmed and edited, and slightly oddball. The Q&A section finds singer Stuart offering advice on how to cope with the first day of school, homoerotic record sleeves and how to cheer up a sad cat.'

It was one thing having the press liking it, but what concerned me more was what the rest of the band thought. Thankfully, it got a universal thumbs-up. So much so that later on that year at the All Tomorrow's Parties festival in Minehead, England, which Belle and Sebastian were curating and performing at, I was asked to introduce the band on stage. It was great to see them all again, and their enthusiasm for the film we had made was obviously nice to hear. I was also told that it had particularly gone down a storm in America.

Back to Minehead though. It was a three-day bill with a great range of artists playing, ranging from Camera Obscura, Steve Mason and The Vaselines, to The Zombies, Isobel Campbell & Mark Lanegan, and Vashti Bunyan.

I travelled there with some mates from London who were intent on drinking the place dry. We were all staying in a chalet, as the venue was a Butlin's holiday complex, which is the best way to have a festival, I believe. Tents, in comparison, are awful. Actually, tents are awful without comparison.

Anyway, we brought a lot of drink with us and the fridge

was frustratingly well-stocked. Frustratingly so, because I had work to do at the festival: not just introduce the band on stage but also, at his request, conduct an interview with Stuart in front of a live audience about his new book and the band in general. I quickly decided that if I had hangovers during all of this then so be it, there was too much fun to be had.

I have to admit though, I was a tad apprehensive about introducing the band on stage. I had never done such a thing and it was paramount in my mind that brevity was the key. No one was there to see me and so I needed to get on and off sharpish, all the time in front of the largest crowd of the weekend. What surprised me though was the mass round of applause that greeted me as I made my way up to the microphone, which, although welcoming, didn't distract me from my mantra: 'brevity is the key'.

I wore the same clothes as I had for the film: black Sta-Prest trousers; white shirt, tie and dark olive-green suit jacket. Without faffing, I launched into my introduction – "Ladies and gentlemen, the time is upon us. The band are ready (cheers from the crowd), you, the audience, appear to be ready (more cheers), please welcome to the stage, the curators and headliners of Bowlie 2, Belle and Sebastian!" More cheers followed as I exited the stage and proceeded to watch the band I had always been a fan of, but had now worked with.

In hindsight, I feel very proud at what we did. In the beginning, it was very much a case of Stuart having a vague artistic vision. It was as much about what it shouldn't have been as what it could be, and we all pulled it off.

I brought what I do well to the table, as did everyone else, and it all seemed to work in the way intended – and that was the most gratifying thing of all. It showed that, with some imagination, you can find new ways in which to promote a new product, while doing it in a way that is both artistic and entertaining. It also looked, as I've said, very cool indeed – and that should never be sniffed at.

12

THE POLYMATH'S PREDICAMENT

The reason why I began to describe myself as a polymath was that I was becoming frustrated trying to describe to people what I did succinctly, as it was proving increasingly difficult to do so.

At various points in my career, I have been called a television presenter, writer, comedian, film-maker, actor, live host and pundit. That all seems very long-winded to trot out when asked the simple question: "What do you do?" in a social situation. I can't exactly pass out copies of my CV or biography, although if it was socially acceptable, I wouldn't have a problem doing so – I have ready access to a printer.

I decided that I needed just one word to concisely answer the query and, after some consideration, 'polymath' it was. It wasn't literally correct though. If a polymath is defined as 'someone of wide knowledge or learning', I feel I would be something of a charlatan in claiming to be one. I do believe I have a fairly comprehensive knowledge on some things, an adequate knowledge of others and little to nothing about a whole lot more.

If, however, I was to take today's more popular connotation of the word, that of someone who is something of an expert in several fields, then it sits easier with me. Admittedly, it's still not entirely true. I would never claim to be an expert on anything, more as someone who is adaptable and can work well in various areas. Having said that, if I were to be labelled an expert, I wouldn't have a problem with it, and would probably add it to the CV before printing out an initial run of 50.

There are certainly some advantages to being labelled a polymath. It's a very handy description to utilise if you find yourself in between jobs. No one likes having to say, "Well, I'm not actually working at the moment," as it can rock one's self-esteem to the very core. By saying, "I'm something of a polymath," it can immediately create the impression that you're always doing something, even when you're not.

It also rolls off the tongue with ease, while, to my ears at least, sounding a tad exotic and intriguing. It's certainly preferable to the other option I toyed with, that of 'Renaissance Man'. That was never going to fly. It would only serve to increase the chances of receiving a punch to the face for being pretentious and deluded in equal measure. I could see it now, "You're a Renaissance Man? Renaissance this!" followed by a swift left hook. I still think there is an idea in there though for some form of artistic superhero: "Renaissance Man – will rid the world of evil but still have time to paint in watercolour." It may be an idea I should write an outline for, regardless of the fact Danny DeVito has already starred in a film with the same name (it's not as good as *Twins* by the way).

Unfortunately, there are some potential downsides to one's status as a polymath. It is all very well being able to turn your hand to various skills but the danger is that you may struggle to be known for excelling at one discipline in particular, and, as a direct consequence, never be the 'go to guy' for anything.

Another is due to the fact that, on declaring yourself a polymath to people, you will often be met with one of two responses, neither of which are particularly satisfying. The first is, "What's a polymath?" which, I have already found, has left me having to explain the literal dictionary definition, the various modern-day connotations and then listing all the different roles I've taken throughout the years as justification for the status. This is very time-consuming for everyone concerned. The second response is, "Are you? Since when?" to which the response, "Since I decided not to say I'm in between jobs, fuckface!" should never be used, regardless of how tempting it may be.

A further problem is that you can develop a kind of identity crisis. Everyone needs an identity, it's imperative. A dentist will wake up in the morning and go to the surgery, a lawyer will go to court and the fireman will clock in at the station. They all know where they should be and what they should be doing from one day to the next. Not so the polymath. You may know where you are going on a Monday but no clue as to what Tuesday holds, let alone the rest of the week. As a consequence, any feeling of consistency or progress can be severely inhibited. You are an outsider in some ways, never quite knowing your place. A modern-day L'Étranger.

I was never told this, of course, I had to find out for myself. It's not as if I set out with the express intention of having multiple roles, it was borne from necessity. If there was no work going in one field, I had to find it in another. It wasn't a case of spreading myself too thinly, it was simply maximising my talents across several platforms. That all goes with the territory, of course. It's simply all in a day's work for a certain certain type of person – The Polymath.

13

UNEXPECTED ENCOUNTERS

Over the years, I have been lucky enough to meet and work with people I greatly respect, and these meetings can inspire, entertain and even have an odd backstory at times. No problem with that, of course, as it all adds to life's rich tapestry whilst also providing further anecdotes, which though conveyed in print format, would probably also work just as well in an audiobook environment, should the opportunity arise.

Working with Bob Monkhouse

When it comes to bona fide legends, it's hard to see past the late Bob Monkhouse. As a performer, his skills in ad-libbing and improvisation were more than a match, not just for his contemporaries, but also for those who would follow him into the worlds of comedy and entertainment in the decades that followed.

Aside from writing and performing, he remained a fervent fan and devotee of film and comedy throughout his life. His vast personal collection of rare films and compendium of joke books are stuff of legend, all the more so due to the latter famously being stolen in 1995 and then returned 18 months later, on the back of a £10,000 reward.

My first memory of seeing him was when he hosted *Family Fortunes*. Of course, he hosted many quiz shows throughout his career, including *The Golden Shot*, *Celebrity Squares* and *Wipeout*, and to some that's all he was, a quiz-show host. This is wholly inaccurate, as he did much more in a career that proved as varied as it was successful.

In his early days, Bob was predominantly a writer, with early examples of his work found in *The Beano* and *The Dandy* comics. He then teamed up with his one-time writing partner, Denis Goodwin, to provide jokes for the comedians and stars of the day, ranging from Arthur Askey and Max Miller, to Bob Hope and even Frank Sinatra.

Although these writing jobs kept him in money, they didn't immediately lead to fame. He would, however, eventually became a household name via those numerous quiz shows, as host of *Sunday Night At The London Palladium* and as an actor in British films such as *Carry On Sergeant* in 1958 and *Dentist In The Chair* in 1960. Bob would also continue to perform stand-up throughout his career, thus helping to cement his reputation with many of today's comedians as something of a godfather figure.

So, to my personal experience of working with Bob. In my second-ever TV job, I bagged the role as roving reporter on the BBC programme *The Bob Monkhouse*

DIY Film Show. As the title suggests, the show looked at all aspects of 'do it yourself' film-making, as well as interviewing directors, actors and producers. This really was a dream job for me, as: firstly, I have always been a massive film fan; secondly, I got my first job in television on the back of a short film I had made and, thirdly, I had the chance to meet Bob Monkhouse.

The bulk of my filming was done independently with a separate crew, as I was at a film premiere one minute and then at a film festival the next, whereas Bob was at different locations filming his links. Luckily, there was to be one day when we were both filming at the same location.

Due to the intensity of the day's shoot, I didn't get a chance to speak to him until lunchtime when, thanks to a producer who knew I was a fan, I was placed next to him at the dinner table. Nervously, I quickly introduced myself but Bob immediately put me at ease and said the pleasure was all his, which was a very kind gesture on his part. For the following half an hour, we chatted or, more precisely, Bob chatted and I intently listened.

What struck me most was his vast knowledge of film. I could have listened to his anecdotes for weeks, although trying to recall all the details now is slightly difficult, as I think I must have been in a bit of a daze at the time.

I do remember spending a good while discussing Jack Nicholson and, in particular, the film, *As Good As It Gets*, which Bob was a big fan of, along with wife Jackie who was also present. He also told me a story of a film in which a scene was to be shot depicting a blustery autumnal day, with the colourful tree leaves on the branches adding to the beauty of the shot. As the scene was being shot in the dead of winter, the director insisted on artificially painted leaves being stuck to all the trees.

This hugely painstaking process would almost have been worth it had they not all been blown off by the wind machine on full blast, the minute the director called, "Action!" Alas, I cannot recall the title of the movie but I imagine the director felt a tad foolish.

At the end of lunch, Bob decided to go to his trailer, and I saw this as a chance to fulfil a promise to my father. When I received the news that I would be working with Bob, my dad had mentioned that he had a Bob Monkhouse book and, if I ever got the chance for Bob to sign it, he would be most grateful. As Bob made his way to the trailer, I saw it as my window of opportunity. Luckily, I had the book on my person along with a good-quality pen. As Bob had left the table shortly before me, I had to be quick, but succeeded in catching up with him and, with a cursory clearing of the throat, asked if he would do the necessary.

I was worried that I might not be the first to have put in such a request that day, but if I was just the latest in a long line of fans craving a signature, Bob certainly never let on. He was pleased to sign a copy of *Over The Limit: My Secret Diaries 1993–8*, but it wasn't until reading the message he had left some moments later that the true character of the man became even more apparent. The message he wrote read, *For Ian – my life is in your hands. Hope this book makes you smile – (from the author, a friend of Douglas) Bob Monkhouse. 30:5:00.*

It was with obvious sadness that I heard the news of Bob's death in December 2003, although it wasn't a great surprise as he had been battling cancer for some time. It was testament to the man that he kept performing as much as his body would let him, while all the time his mind and wit remained as sharp as ever.

In the subsequent years since his passing, I'm glad he is increasingly viewed as a great comedian and writer and not just a quiz-show host – not that there should be any stigma attached to presenting such formats if you do it as well as he did. He made it look alarmingly easy, and that just serves to accentuate the supreme quality of his performing skills.

There are many words which would contribute to an adequate description of Bob – comedian, writer, host, entertainer and actor would all suffice. I would of course also add just one more – friend.

The Strange Case of Jamie Lee Curtis

One of the greatest oddities in my broadcasting career would have to be how my early short films, for the most part made with no budget at all, would come to have a direct correlation with Hollywood and cult television.

One such example involved the actress Jamie Lee Curtis, whom I interviewed as part of a junket in London. As usual, I deviated from the traditional line of questioning and asked about her appearance in an episode of *Columbo* in which she played a particularly gnarly, yet humorous, waitress.

Curtis was excited to talk about it and informed me that it was only her second ever acting job, and that she had never seen it since it originally aired in 1977. This excitement reached fever pitch when I told her I had a copy of it. The reason for this was purely down to my musical explorations, as when I had been recording the song 'Columbo & Coffee', which of course lead to the accompanying video, I was determined to include a sample of Peter Falk speaking. To do this, I recorded from television around 20 episodes of *Columbo*, which at the time was being shown every weekday on BBC2.

If I had recorded one show, it probably would have been enough for the sample, but thankfully I didn't, as episode 17, *The Bye–Bye Sky High I.Q. Murder Case*, featured Ms Curtis. I told her right then that if she fancied, I could send her a copy – to which she immediately wrote down an address in Santa Monica for me to do just that.

I subsequently transferred my old VHS to the US format SVHS, with the help of an editor friend, and wrote an accompanying letter. It didn't occur to me she might rather have a DVD. The letter was all important – so important that I bought expensive paper for it to be written on. It's a basic point, but if a letter is of importance, and this one was, it should always be written or printed on the best quality paper available. It feels good in the hand of the recipient and shows an element of class.

In the letter I detailed how I had made the transfer, how nice it had been to meet her and asked that if she could help me get any work in America through her contacts it would be greatly appreciated. There was no point going to all this trouble without trying to get a leg up, and the fact that her husband is *Spinal Tap*'s Christopher Guest was also a contributing factor for me putting a copy of my own showreel in the package for good measure too.

It was then simply a case of stumping up the cost for the postage and off it went, along with my hopes. I waited. Waited some more, but nothing. I eventually gave up on it and, if it popped back in my mind, I would simply find solace in *True Lies* being a pile of crap.

It came as some surprise then that, when picking up my mail around two months afterwards, I found a letter postmarked California, opened it up and sure enough, Curtis had replied. The handwritten note read as follows:

Douglas,

How sweet of you to remember and go to the extraordinary lengths to get me the tape. I am most grateful. A first for me. As for the American market, I will pass tape on to a friend in TV. Who knows. Best always.

Thanks. xxJ.

I immediately believed *True Lies* to be something of a misunderstood and underrated work. Regardless, it was proof, if it were needed, that you can – for no other reason than because you fancied doing so – write a song about your favourite detective with your mate, and for it to lead to correspondence with a Hollywood star. Strange really when you look at it that way. Incidentally, I think the tape for her TV friend must have got lost in transit.

Face to Face with Dirk Benedict

It's one thing possessing a tape of someone's first forays into screen acting, but interviewing a hero from childhood whom you have impersonated in a short film without their knowledge, is another entirely.

This was the case with *The A–Team*'s Dirk Benedict, aka Face. My friend Milo had written a song called 'The Man Who Listened To Planes', which featured a sample of *The A–Team* theme tune. For the accompanying video, a plot was devised to replicate the show's recurring theme of BA Baracus being scared to fly on planes. Filmed in my flat and at an air show, I would play not just the part of Face, but also Murdock and Hannibal, all the time wearing masks of each of the characters' faces, with Milo, a skinny white boy, taking on the unlikely role of BA.

The filming gave us both a chance to reminisce about the TV programme which was a huge part of our childhood, an era–defining show for sure. Fast-forward a few years, and Dirk was in the UK promoting something or other and I was to interview him. How strange it was, speaking to someone, whilst not being sure if it was wise to bring up the fact that I had once made a mask of his face and played the fictional character he was most famous for in a short film.

When we made the film in Edinburgh, the idea of someone like me meeting someone like him was farcical, and would have seemed like an impossible scenario. Then of course it happened. Surreal. At the age of eight, and with Face being my favourite character from the show, I received a Face action figure and *A–Team* toy van for my birthday. The van actually featured in the short, the doll sadly didn't.

It's understandably exciting meeting famous people or idols from childhood when reporting on a red-carpet event or at a press junket, but to have gone to the lengths of playing them on camera for pure enjoyment, only to meet them a few years later and be able to have a discussion with them about their work is as I said, surreal. I'm just glad I didn't bring up the doll.

14

WHEN REAL LIFE AND SHOW BUSINESS COLLIDE

If we had a choice as to when and where we receive devastating news, it would probably be somewhere private and surrounded by people who could provide support. Obviously, life isn't like that and, unfortunately, we cannot determine when such an occurrence will take place.

One such instance ingrained in my memory took place in December 2003, when I was walking into a screening room to view a film I would be interviewing the principal actors about. My phone rang, I answered it and was duly informed my manager, Jimmy, who had represented me since I got my first job in television, and who was not just an agent but a friend and confidant, was dead.

This was the first time in my life that I had been informed of someone having died who had not been suffering from any illness. It was also a piece of news

I struggled to compute, as I had seen him the previous day and was due to see him later that week – so how could he possibly be dead?

Of course, as I was soon to learn, untimely deaths and logic don't tend to sit well together. It was just a total shock. He had suffered a huge heart attack and died, still only in his mid–40s. Up until this point, I had never had another agent. He had taken me on, shown faith in me and we were building something together. Suddenly, he was gone and I never had a chance to say goodbye to not just my manager, but my friend.

Regrettably, as one journeys through life, such occurrences seem to become more commonplace. But that didn't prepare me for the news I would receive one October day in 2012. I was walking up Great Portland Street in central London on my way to Western House, home of BBC Radio 2 and 6Music. I was to be a guest on Fred MacAuley's BBC Radio Scotland show which, due to the use of an ISDN line, I could appear on live whilst remaining in London. I would be speaking on the subject of television presenting and presenters, subjects I felt qualified to expatiate upon. As I was a little early, I decided to phone my parents for a chat but, unbeknown to me, I was about to be hit with a bombshell. That very morning my father had been diagnosed with cancer.

I stood still on the pavement as I was given the details, feeling like the world should stop, but watching people and traffic moving as normal. After the relatively short conversation, which I had to make sense of in my own mind and which would be continued after my engagement, I made my way into the BBC building.

I decided to still do the show as I was committed but,

while waiting in reception, I didn't feel all there. Understandable of course, but strange nonetheless. One prominent thought in my mind, however, was that the kind of moment you fear in life, the kind that you know will come but never want to contemplate until it does, had arrived. If only I could have been with my father when it did though. Circumstance seldom affords such fortune.

I was obviously in some state of shock but calm enough to believe that going on air was still the only course of action to be taken. I was ushered to a studio, which was completely empty apart from a microphone and a pair of headphones. I spoke to the producer down the line, who informed me they would be coming to me in five minutes.

What a five minutes that was. I simply stared into space and tried to not only take in the information I had received, but also remain focused on the job I had to do. What if I could not physically speak? *Nope, couldn't let that happen,* I thought. The old adage of the show going on, no matter what the circumstances, was prominent in my mind – and I knew my father would want it that way. It was all I could cling onto, in all honesty, as I was introduced and tried to wax lyrical to Fred, his other guests and a listenership who had no idea what I was really thinking about. It would be the most insignificant broadcast I would ever make, yet one I couldn't possibly forget.

To some, it may appear inconceivable to take part in a live national radio show directly after such news but, in truth, it wasn't. I just got on with it, as I didn't have any other option other than to walk away but, for whatever reason, that just didn't seem a viable alternative. I had obviously appeared on many radio shows before, so I wasn't in an alien environment, but I will say this. Being in that studio, waiting to be introduced, felt like the loneliest place in the world. Once on air it was totally manageable, I just had to block everything out for a few minutes until I could leave the studio and begin to decipher what had happened. I spoke to a couple of friends afterwards who had listened to the show, and all were quick to tell me that no one would have had a clue how I was really feeling, as I sounded my usual self. Pulling out at the last minute wouldn't have changed anything, that's for sure.

As I left the building, it coincided with Steven Tyler and Joe Perry from Aerosmith walking in to conduct an interview in another studio. Their sudden appearance was as unexpected as it was inconsequential. I had two things on my mind – first, phone my father and, after that, find the nearest pub and order a stiff drink. This I did, in that order – and then headed home in readiness for the coming months, which would be difficult to say the least culminating in my father's passing some eight months later.

Not long after my father's funeral took place, I dropped in to his local for a pint and had a chat with the barman there, a good chap also called Douglas and whom my dad always enjoyed a laugh and joke with. Whilst toasting my dad at the bar, Dougie asked if it was true, as my dad had told him, that when I interviewed Steven Spielberg my first question to him had been about *Columbo*? Not *Jaws*, *Indiana Jones*, *ET* or *Schindler's List*. *Columbo*. Well, as is probably obvious by now, if there's any chance to bring the great TV show up in conversation, I'm going to take it.

To explain, Spielberg directed the 1971 *Columbo* episode, *Murder By The Book*, which is absolutely one of my favourite episodes and, as Spielberg has said himself, up until that point, it was the finest script he had ever been given to direct, and the closest he had come to making a movie.

It begins with a shot of a car travelling along an LA freeway, only for the camera to pan back and reveal the shot being taken high up on a skyscraper. It isn't dissimilar in some ways to the opening of Francis Ford Coppola's *The Conversation*, filmed three years afterwards, when the camera pans back from a busy city square from a greatly elevated position. It's certainly a captivating way to start the episode and gives a cinematic feel, whilst showcasing Spielberg's vast talents before they were more widely known. I wagered that not many, if anyone, had ever asked him about the shot and it was a great opportunity to show that I knew and respected not just his most famous works, but those apparently long-forgotten. It certainly paid off, as he was more responsive to that than he was about the film he was in London to promote. It seemed he wanted to talk to me for some time about it, something I was very happy to oblige with.

Back to the pub in Edinburgh though. So, Dougie the barman asks if it was true that, when I met Steven Spielberg, the first question I asked him was about *Columbo* as my dad had recounted to him. It was, as it happened, I told Dougie. He responded after a split second and with a huge grin on his face, "that's fucking brilliant!"

That was good enough for me. I knew my father was proud of my efforts, and to picture him regaling the story of his son meeting the world-famous director with a particular line of questioning in his local in Edinburgh made me smile. He got what I was doing and I couldn't ask for more than that. The fact that Dougie the barman did, as well, could only be viewed as an extra bonus.

15

SHORT-FILM MAKERS OF THE WORLD, UNITE AND TAKE OVER

There are all manner of books and websites on how to make short films, which can scare a prospective film-maker off before any shooting commences. In some instances, it would seem impossible to achieve if you don't have fancy equipment and a great deal of money to burn. Balls to that, I say. Whilst the technology used may change, the pursuit of good storytelling stays the same. With some ingenuity, persistence, and the odd bit of luck along the way, much can be accomplished – from an initial idea to the finished piece. When I set out to make the short film *Timber!* I knew it wouldn't be easy, but I was willing to put the work in to make it happen. This is the story of that process, which hopefully shows that it is possible to make a film, albeit a short, without bankruptcy.

The initial idea for the film came to me when musing over some of my own, and indeed my friends', good and bad luck with love. It struck me that, while many, many films have been written on the subject, they always seem to have happy endings and a positive (if not entirely realistic) resolution. Even in a film such as *(500) Days Of Summer*, where it appears it will end on a downer (mild spoiler alert), the protagonist meets Autumn, and we are led to believe that she will be the girl for him and they will both live happily thereafter.

Conversely, I wanted to write something in which the story ended on a laugh, but this didn't necessarily mean the protagonist got the girl. I also had certain thoughts floating around my mind, such as the well-known idea that the more we live, the more we realise that life, for better or worse, doesn't pan out the way you fully intended or expected. This was something I wanted to explore.

I was conscious that many of the short films I had done in the past had been out-and-out comedy and satire. I really enjoyed making such films as *The Anti–Fantastic Campaign* or *The Skills Of Conversation: The Heartburn Pause*, but it was time for a change. The prospect of still using comedy but also including some pathos and human emotion was something I felt compelled to do.

Scripting

After consolidating my ideas into a first-draft script, I was eager to film a test version of what I had, with whoever I could get on board. This would help determine what worked, what didn't and, if possible, what new ideas and dialogue could be prised from such a practice. With a friend operating the camera, I set aside a Sunday afternoon to do just that. I also roped in my flatmates to play the other roles.

After filming this rough read-through/rehearsal, I indeed had new ideas to include in the script and a clearer mind as to what to purge. It's an invaluable process and I would highly recommend it to those who have a first-draft script and want to hone it down. It's far better to do this than assemble a cast and crew and start filming, whilst all the time having a few nagging doubts about your script.

Funding

This was always going to be a big headache as I simply didn't have enough money to fund the film myself. Due to the fact I wanted it to have excellent production qualities (or as excellent as I could possibly muster), to hire a crew and equipment would cost a fortune.

I did look into the official channels to acquire funding, but it became quickly apparent there would be a lot of paperwork and absolutely no guarantee of acquiring any money, after what would, undoubtedly, be a long wait.

As someone once said to me, "If a story is worth telling, you'll find a way to tell it." I thought my story was – and, with that, was determined to prove it. I also didn't have the patience to hang around with dwindling hope for funding, and so decided to try and pull in as many favours as possible from as many people who were willing to help.

Crew

This is where I got very lucky. In 2008 I had been working on the Channel 4 show, the *Red Bull Air Race*, with a great crew with whom I got on very well. During the filming, which took us all over the world, there was a lot of time spent in hotel lobbies, airport departure lounges and indeed on long-haul flights. During this time, I talked at length with two chaps who quickly turned from work colleagues to friends. The first was Stevie Haywood, who would become the soundman and sound editor on *Timber!* We spoke for long periods about film, music and many other things besides. I showed him a couple of shorts I had already done and he was impressed. This was also the case when I showed them to Charlie Grainger, who was also working on the show as chief cameraman. Aside from the programme we were working on, Charlie and Stevie had worked with Chris Morris, Shane Meadows and on HBO's *Band of Brothers*. This obviously impressed me greatly, but more importantly, was further proof of their experience and talent, which was clearly evident in the way they went about their work.

They both said that if I was ever planning on doing another short in the future, they would help me out by doing the sound and vision, as well as supplying the equipment. This was such a kind gesture and, as I say, a massive stroke of luck on my part. It meant we would be shooting on a DVCPro HD camera, along with professional sound gear and lights, when the time eventually came to make the film. When it did, we had to juggle filming around our paid gigs, but we managed to set aside shooting dates when we were all free. I was greatly indebted to them, as it would have been very difficult otherwise and certainly not nearly as much fun.

Actors

Again, this is where my connections came in handy. I became the film's protagonist as, not only did it seem the easiest way to do things, but it was a story I had written and I wanted to tell it first-hand. However, it still left me with many other roles to cast. It was a no-brainer to get Miles involved and, through him, I got the numbers of some acquaintances of his who were also actors. Through those, I got the names of even more actors, so there were a few possibilities as to who to cast. What worried me was the fact that I had no money to pay anybody, which I thought could be a sticking point.

It was then Miles said something to me that gave me the confidence to believe I could get all the thespians I needed. He reminded me that actors want to act as much as possible and, due to the nature of the job, there's a lot of time when they aren't working. If they are offered a part in a short and they like the script, they are more than likely to say yes. This proved to be the case and I filled all the slots.

Filming

My intention was to film all the pieces to camera on the roof of my flat on the first day, which involved detailing certain thoughts on love and relationships straight into the lens. That way, at least, it would feel like a productive start and we would have the skeleton of the film, which all the sketches and other sequences would branch off from, in the can.

I succeeded in doing this, even though there was a gardener nearby intent on using a leaf-blower, which buggered up our sound on a couple of takes, until he thankfully moved on. Due to the fact I was the only one appearing in front of camera that day, it wasn't too stressful, and I only had to concern myself with the two-man crew of Stevie and Charlie being fed, watered and happy with everything.

I knew it would be more difficult when dealing with the other actors, crew members and various locations on future shooting days. While this proved to be the case, I always managed to get things sorted in the end. The first thing I had to do was secure days with Stevie and Charlie, as without them nothing could be done.

There was one day when Charlie couldn't make it but I couldn't get the actors I needed on any other date. Due to this potential problem, I called on the services of Josh Eve, a cameraman I was working with at the time on another job. Not only was Josh good with a camera and a great bloke, he had also toured with The Beta Band as their film projectionist. This was all he had to have on the CV, as they are of course one of my favourite bands of all time.

My HQ through all of this was my desk in my bedroom, where phone calls and emails were made and sent to everyone concerned, until I was eventually able to settle on a shooting schedule. There were times when it seemed I might only be able to shoot one scene in a day, which would have been a waste of Stevie and Charlie's time. But, by hook or by crook, I filled up the days with as many scenes to film as possible. Nothing was shot in sequence, with the final day being taken up by the dinner-party scene, which was filmed on a boiling-hot summer's afternoon in my living room – with us all inside and the curtains drawn. I had to buy quite a few bin liners to black out the windows on that one, but it worked out well.

With regard to the locations I used, it was simply a case

of asking permission, whilst assuring those in charge that we wouldn't take up too much time. For example, we shot in a pub at 10am before it opened to the public. The pints used in that scene were full of 100% proper lager and I had a slightly light head by 10.30am. To give another example, a scene featuring my character playing golf was shot at the pitch-and-putt course in Queen's Park, North London. I simply told the guy in charge that what I was filming was an independent venture and that we would only be there for a short while. He was fine with that and let us in.

My biggest concern throughout filming was with the sequence intended to be shot immediately outside St Pancras station. This was integral to the whole story and if we didn't get it, there would be no pay-off at the end. We set out to St Pancras on the penultimate filming day, with me quietly worrying in the back of Charlie's van. I was stressing that due to security measures, we might be forced to stop filming or told to get a permit. It also concerned me that I was going to look suspicious. I would have to walk into the station, acting as if I was about to hop on the Eurostar, then quickly take my jacket off and unravel my shirt to look like I was on my way back from Paris (where my character had gone in a last-ditch attempt to find the love of his life). I would then have to walk out again and pass the camera, which would remain in the same position.

With all that in mind, we arrived at King's Cross, got out the van and started to film. I remember seeing policemen and station workers everywhere and knowing that if we got just one decent take, we could get going. As it turned out, nobody batted an eyelid, with at one point a policeman walking straight past us, not giving the slightest query as to what we were up to. In the end, we did three takes with slightly different angles so there was a variety of choice. We then went to the pub, as it was a huge relief to know we now had the conclusion of the film in the bag.

Editing

By pulling in the contacts of Stevie and Charlie, I was able to acquire the services of an editor who they had not only worked with, but was also a friend of theirs. The fortuitous thing was that Doug Oliphant was wanting to break into more comedic/dramatic work, and so saw the experience of editing *Timber!* as a useful one. I saw it as getting in a great editor for free, who had access to a professional edit suite, was superb at his job and wanted to edit my film.

We worked late into the evenings when the edit suite was free, and up until we needed to get the last train home. We would have hired a taxi but we couldn't really afford to, as our homes were in North London and the edit suite was in Richmond. I didn't mind getting the train as long as I had my music to listen to and a book to read – the simple, yet important, pleasures.

Music

It's imperative to use original music if you want to get into film festivals or be shown by broadcasters. There are many tunes I would like to have used by several artists, such as the Stevie Jackson-penned Belle and Sebastian song, 'The Wrong Girl', over the closing titles, or selected cuts by Bob Lind, Nick Garrie, Jeffrey Lewis and many others besides. This was not possible, however, as the money to use such tracks wasn't there – and so I called on my friend, John Reynolds.

John and I have been friends since we met as fresh-faced 18-year-olds and played in bands, both together and apart, in Edinburgh. After I moved to London, John continued to work, both in groups and in music production, amassing an impressive musical output. A few months before we started filming, he sent me a batch of new songs he had recorded. I thought they were great and knew they would fit the film well. I then asked John if I could use them, and he was kind enough to say yes. I also snuck in 'Columbo & Coffee', of course.

The graphics used to accompany the music in the opening and closing titles came courtesy of Scott Walker. Another friend from Edinburgh, Scott is an excellent graphic designer, and was voted Digital Professional of the Year at The Herald Scottish Digital Business Awards in 2014. In this case, he simply wanted to help. I'm glad he did, as they finished things off nicely.

Epilogue

So eventually everything was done and *Timber!* had progressed from the seed of an idea to the finished article. It's certainly gratifying to have accomplished what I set out to do, and I'm glad to say the feedback was positive. As is always the case with such creative undertakings, if I was to do it all over again, I would make a few tweaks but, overall, was pretty happy with the outcome.

I entered it for a couple of festivals (Edinburgh and Raindance) but it didn't make it to final selection. I would have entered it for more, but the price of simply getting it considered by each festival – as much as £50 a time – was just too expensive. Instead, I opted for a distribution deal I was offered by Shorts International and, as a result, it was shown in the USA and Europe, whilst earning me some money in royalties.

What was equally as pleasing was the reaction from the cast and members of the public alike – everyone who saw it seemed to like it. I received many emails from people, empathising with what to them seemed to be a more realistic, albeit at times comical, portrayal of the search for love in today's society. Perhaps it was because I put myself out there and on the line a bit. Some people aren't too comfortable talking about their love lives in the pub, never mind seeing it on screen. I'm firmly in the Woody Allen camp when it comes to sharing lessons learned from my personal life, just with a slightly smaller budget and profile, and a few less Academy Awards.

16

THE GREATEST TV SERIES YOU'LL NEVER SEE

Developing ideas can be a hellish process, whether it be for television or the movies. A lot of stop-start, false promise, hope, encouragement, expectation and then, more often than not, rejection and dejection. For film fans, books such as David Hughes's *Tales From Development Hell: The Greatest Movies Never Made?* and Simon Braund's *The Greatest Movies You'll Never See: Unseen Masterpieces by The World's Greatest Directors* deal with such issues in Hollywood.

I too have been through 'development hell', although it wasn't in Hollywood, sadly. I was employed for two weeks to work up some new ideas for a London-based production company. I basically sat in an office for a fortnight, racking my brains for inspiration but only coming up with stuff that, at best, I felt was not far enough detached from 'a bit shite'. It was a most dispiriting experience, and I was close to telling the company that I would forgo my payment, as I didn't think my work merited it. I was seriously going to do just that, until I spoke to another pal of mine, also working in development at another production company. He told me, in no uncertain terms, not to reject payment and that what I was going through was what 99% of those working in development go through 99% of the time. One thing was obvious, it wasn't an area I was destined to be working in and, after my two weeks were up, I took the money and ran.

That experience didn't stop me working up ideas I thought were good, however, in no small part down to the fact that I could do so in my own time, out of an office and under no pressure to justify a weekly wage. Admittedly, my ideas – which mostly involved music and film – didn't get taken up by any channels. I was always told they were too niche or that such shows simply do not rate highly enough with audiences.

However, I'm sure most people whose job it is to develop ideas for television shows will always have one idea that they thought was a sure-fire winner and deserved to be made, even though, along with thousands of others, it never will. I am no different. My idea would stem from one of my greatest passions – football grounds.

Since I visited my first in 1983 as a very young boy, I have been somewhat in awe of football stadiums. I was taken along with my father and grandfather to see Hibernian play Aberdeen at Easter Road Stadium in Edinburgh on a cold October afternoon. Before the teams even took to the field, I was already marvelling at the massed banks of terracing, floodlights and even the electronic scoreboard – which didn't work and would never work on all my return visits, of which there were many. It was actually a strange introduction to football, as Hibs won 2–1 against an Aberdeen side managed by Alex Ferguson, who were at the time the European Cup Winners' Cup holders.

I was to quickly find out that seeing Hibs win wasn't a regular experience, but you have your team and you stick with them through thin and thinner. As I always say, being a Hibs and Scotland fan from an early age helps to harden your skin for the inevitable disappointments later life can throw at you.

Only two years later, I would again see the two teams play one another, but this time it was in the League Cup Final at Hampden Park, Glasgow. As far as the the actual game was concerned, it could only be described as an unmitigated disaster. Inside the first 12 minutes, Hibs were two-nil down and would go on to lose three-nil. This was obviously extremely disappointing for me and the many, many thousands of others who had travelled through from Edinburgh.

However, on the plus side, the national stadium was a breathtaking sight to behold. It was no longer the biggest in the world, as it had been before the Maracana was redeveloped in Brazil, but to a small child's eyes (and I'm sure a great many adult ones as well) it still looked mightily impressive.

It was huge, foreboding even, but totally captivating, and the details all around intrigued me. The height of the floodlights, the massive roof covering one terrace behind the goal, the press box on top of the main stand, which seemed to hang there regardless of the laws of gravity, the crush barriers on the terracing and the stanchions attached to the goalposts.

This childlike excitement has never really dissipated over the years, as I have visited stadiums all around the world – many times just to look at them from the outside – before scuttling off to find a record shop if there was one. I was certain about one thing though – there was a show in this.

It was then, with a sense of excitement and purpose, that I sat down and began to work on a series idea that would combine sport, social history and architectural design to great effect. I spent a long time on the pitch document, which included show outlines, spin-off series and even saw me saving it as a PDF file – that's how seriously I was taking it. Alas, like most ideas pitched, it was not taken up. The broadcaster in question, the BBC, with whom it felt right to make such a series, passed on it. I swore a bit that day, I can tell you, and then had a few drinks, which only facilitated in making the cursing more voluminous.

Regardless, and in the spirit of the Hughes and Braund books, I would like to share my idea as – and I know I'm bound to say this – I still think it's a belter. It's a fairly lengthy pitch document running to a few pages, but I think it just goes to show how into the idea I was and indeed what is required by channel commissioners. You might be able to write the gist of a show on the back of a fag packet but, for a full-on proposal, you'll need a few A4 sheets. So, without further ado, I give you the finalised pitch document of one of the greatest TV series never made – *Cathedrals For The Masses*.

Cathedrals For The Masses

A journey into the world of the football stadium – a place of worship for millions

Of all the buildings in the public realm, stadiums enjoy the highest profile – millions of people across the world worship at them every week, far more than can be found attending churches. But what do we really know about them? What are the stories behind them? What do they mean to us? From the pioneering work of the first great stadium designer, Archibald Leitch, to the architect of the new Wembley, Norman Foster. We will discover who built them, why there is relatively little known about the architects themselves, and why their creations are so special to fans, architects and communities alike.

Taking us on this journey around the UK is Douglas Anderson, who will meet those who have built stadiums, those who play at them and the supporters who regularly inhabit them.

WHAT MAKES A STADIUM SPECIAL?

Today the football ground can be regarded as among the most important buildings a city possesses. The stadium is much more than just steel framework, bricks and mortar – it embodies a club's history, many of its major triumphs and disasters, and is often as familiar to the fan as his or her local high street, while providing a focus for the community. On a global scale, they act as symbols for a city, region or even a nation.

Their architectural features can be viewed in the same light as a cathedral and can cause as much controversy as the latest modern sculpture to be discussed and dissected in the media. In recent history, such celebrated architectural feats as The Gherkin building in London, the Scottish Parliament building in Edinburgh and the Millennium Centre in Cardiff ultimately lack the profound effect the stadium architects continue to have on the Britons who inhabit their structures. They are seen by many more on television in all corners of the planet, but what is the continuing story of the stadium? It is now time for that to be examined, investigated and celebrated.

WHAT ARE WE GOING TO SEE THROUGHOUT THE SERIES?

For the first time, we take an affectionate look at stadiums through the eyes of architects, historians, footballers, famous fans and the season-ticket holders to gain an insight into what makes these buildings so distinctive, significant and cherished.

SERIES STRUCTURE

The structure of the series will be defined by geography, using a similar template showcased in the BBC Show *Comedy Map of Britain*. By using this framework, it enables numerous strands to be included in the programme, from the sporting and artistic to the sociological and political.

Show 1– Scotland – The natural place to start. At one stage, Glasgow could boast the three biggest stadiums in the world (Hampden, Ibrox and Celtic Park). It was also the birthplace of Archibald Leitch, the pioneer of British stadium design. Further east, Edinburgh was where Douglas Anderson was born and visited his first football ground.

Show 2 – The North West of England – incorporating Old Trafford, Maine Road/Etihad Stadium, Anfield and Goodison Park. An area where some of the most celebrated clubs in the land play at world-renowned stadiums. In the case of Manchester United, their unofficial ground name 'The Theatre of Dreams' is almost as famous as their official one.

Show 3 – London and the South East – incorporating Highbury/Emirates Stadium, White Hart Lane, Stamford Bridge and Wembley. The capital houses perhaps the most famous stadium of them all – Wembley. It is also a city where tradition and modern development have converged, most notably in the case of Arsenal and their move from Highbury to the Emirates.

Show 4 – The North East and Yorkshire – incorporating St James' Park, Roker Park/Stadium of Light, Ayresome Park/Riverside Stadium, Elland Road, Bramall Lane and Hillsborough Stadium. The view that a stadium is at the heart of the community is perhaps best exemplified in the North East and, in particular Newcastle, where the stadium is situated in the city centre. Heading south to Yorkshire, we find Hillsborough, a ground which will forever be remembered for disaster and the political and social ramifications that followed.

Show 5 – The Midlands – Villa Park, St Andrew's, The Hawthorns, Molineux Stadium, the Baseball Ground/ Pride Park/iPro Stadium, Meadow Lane and The City Ground. The second city was home to one of the most traditional and artistically preserved stadiums in the land – Villa Park. It has since been redeveloped but what has been lost and gained? The Midlands is also home to the oldest club in the football league – Notts

County, thereby giving them the longest stadium history.

Show 6 – Wales, The South West and Northern Ireland – Millennium Stadium, Vetch Field/Liberty Stadium, Ninian Park, Ashton Gate Stadium, Windsor Park and The Oval. In stadium evolution, Cardiff has been at the forefront, so much so that during Wembley's redevelopment, it became the destination for English fans attending cup finals. This is the end of our journey and a time to review what we have discovered and what can be concluded.

AREAS OF INTEREST

Although geography helps to define the narrative structure of the show, there is a broad range of subject matter to be examined and which will be interspersed throughout the series. This includes:

Architecture

Who built the stadiums in the UK?

Why are these designers still relatively unknown to the general public?

Where are the greatest grounds and why?

Which stadiums are listed buildings?

An examination of the stadium pioneers such as Archibald Leitch, whose work was showcased at, amongst other grounds, Old Trafford, Hampden Park, Anfield, Ibrox and Goodison Park.

Can stadiums really be viewed in the same way as

cathedrals or town halls? Have modern stadiums lost character? Do they all look the same?

What else have stadium architects designed? For example, Populous – the world's leading sports architecture firm – have designed the Emirates and the Macron Stadium (Bolton, formerly known as the Reebok Stadium), as well as many other sporting stadia around the world. They have also completed 180 fairground projects and the O2 Arena in Dublin, showing their expertise in non-sporting environments.

What influence have British designers had on European stadiums?

Sociological

What makes a ground special?

Why did certain areas of stadiums produce better atmospheres than others? Eg, 'The Shelf' at White Hart Lane, 'The Shed' at Stamford Bridge or 'The Jungle' at Celtic Park.

The idea of grounds being a place for worship. Just as families used to attend church, they now attend football grounds in far greater numbers.

The Roman Colosseum – the prototype for every football ground. A place where people would go to watch gladiators do battle, as opposed to two teams fighting it out on a football field.

The price of building a new football ground meaning that the fans who have been following their team for years are priced out.

Psychological

Intimidation factor – grounds as fortresses and the psychology around it.

The design of a ground helping/hindering the effect on the referee. This is examined in the Salford University research paper *How stadium design affects football results*, and details that if fans are further away from the pitch due to a running track, they are unable to exert as much psychological pressure on the referee than if they were closer.

Political

Political legislation and acts passed for ground safety, such as the Taylor Report, and the instances that were the catalyst for them e.g. Heysel, Hillsborough and Bradford.

Interviews with fans of stadiums

Interviews with fans, famous and otherwise, about what a particular stadium means to them. For example, Michael Palin (known to have a secret passion for stadia), Noel Gallagher (who achieved his ambition of playing at his beloved Manchester City's Maine Road and the Etihad) and those who have visited every Football League ground in the country, known collectively as 'groundhoppers'.

Fan Footage

As well as using the extensive BBC archive, there will also be the possibility for viewer-generated content. This could be in the form of fans sending in their own pictures and videos of grounds, something many already do by posting on YouTube.

Disappearing Stadia

Where were the grounds that have now disappeared, to be replaced by supermarkets and housing developments?

Non-Sporting Events

Stadiums used for non-sporting events – papal masses, rallies by Winston Churchill, Billy Graham's evangelical crusades, and rock concerts.

Stadium statistics

Including capacities, highest attendances for club/ national matches and stadium forerunners, such as the first ground to have floodlights.

STYLE

Cathedrals For The Masses incorporates some of the elements of several of the BBC's most successful shows but takes the viewer to newer areas. Fans of architecture, sport and history will all be able to enjoy this programme. In the way *Who Do You Think You Are?* looks at family history, *Cathedrals For The Masses* tells the story of millions of people's shared history and experiences through football grounds. Furthermore, by using the *Who Do You Think You Are?* template, it will help in discovering information about stadium architects from the past of whom little is known to the public at large. Another highly acclaimed BBC show, *Restoration*, championed buildings which had fallen into disrepair and celebrated their worth. *Cathedrals For*

The Masses champions not just old grounds that fell into disrepair and vanished, but also those restored and redeveloped into new and stunning structures. Visually, there is also the opportunity to employ similar techniques used in *Comedy Connections/Movie Connections* and the aforementioned *Comedy Map Of Britain*.

TALENT

Douglas Anderson's own fascination with grounds began at the first match he attended at Easter Road Stadium, the home of Hibernian in 1983. It had a profound effect on him and ignited a passionate interest in football stadia as strong today as it was then. Since his footballing baptism at Easter Road, he has visited many grounds, both in the UK and around the world, and often when there is no game being played.

SPIN-OFF

As there is such a wealth of subject matter, in the UK and abroad, the first series and subsequent series would take the following structure –

Series 1 – Football stadiums in the UK

Series 2 – Football stadiums in Europe

Series 3 – Football stadiums in South America and Asia

Series 4 – Non-football stadiums throughout the world, incorporating sports such as rugby, cricket and baseball

It would also be proposed that the author of various books on football grounds, Simon Inglis, would be brought in as a consultant on the show to help in maintaining the required level of authenticity. There would also be the possibility of a book spin-off from the series, thus increasing the show's commercial potential.

Additionally, there is much room for interactivity via the show's website. Viewers would be encouraged to contribute to the programme's discussion groups. The topics could include stadium stories, first visits, most stadiums visited and the best/worst in the country.

EXAMPLE SHOW OUTLINE:

SHOW 2 – THE NORTH WEST

Our journey to this hotbed of football culture will see us meet managers, players from the past and present, historians, architects, famous fans and even religious figures. Throughout, we will see archive footage of stadiums supplied by fans and from the clubs' own extensive libraries. We will also, of course, see goals that coincide with the timeframes being examined. We will deal with the themes of sporting/social/political history and change, architecture, community and people's shared pride and passion for their unofficial second homes.

Our first port of call is the biggest club ground of them all, Old Trafford – the home to the most famous team in the land, Manchester United. It has also appeared in more feature films than any other British ground, including *Charlie Bubbles*, starring Albert Finney (1967), *Hell Is A City,* with Stanley Baker and Donald Pleasence (1960), *Billy Liar,* starring Tom Courtenay and Julie Christie (1963) and *The Lovers!* with Richard Beckinsale and Paula Wilcox (1973). Here we will speak to Alex Ferguson and find out what the stadium means to him and what effect it had on his players. We will also find out what memories he has of visiting grounds as a young fan and how they have changed, for the better and for worse.

We will further examine the history of the ground and a club who, in 1910, were christened 'Moneybags United', due in part to other people's jealousy as, in one writer's words, Old Trafford was 'a wonder to behold'. It had a billiard room, massage room, a gymnasium, a plunge bath, a capacity of 80,000 and attendants to lead patrons to their five-shilling tip-up seats from the tea rooms. We will investigate which of these features still exist, such as the original players' tunnel, preserved in memory of the players who once walked down it, although it's no longer used.

We will discover why Old Trafford was a trendsetter in stadium architecture. In 1964, the United Road stand cover was taken down to be replaced by a cantilever, designed by the brilliantly named Manchester firm of architects, Mather and Nutter, who later went on to design stands at Molineux and White Hart Lane. The United Road stand was seen as a trendsetter for three main reasons, all of which we will delve into. Firstly, it allowed for expansion at either end. Secondly, it recognised the spectators' preference for both standing and seated accommodation but, thirdly, and most important of all, it incorporated the first private boxes ever seen at a British football ground. To persuade the United directors, Mather and Nutter took them to the Manchester Racecourse to see the private boxes they had installed there, and eventually convinced them that the football fraternity would welcome such a luxury just as much as the racing one.

We will further explore the same company of architects, later renamed Atherden Fuller, who in subsequent years suggested that the club build a museum to celebrate their history. The museum, which opened in May 1986, was believed to be the first of its kind at any club ground in the world. We will take a tour of this and see the images of how the stadium has gone from strength to strength.

We will then speak to the team's most celebrated current players and find out what their first impressions of the stadium were on arrival and what it is like playing there. We then move on to the unsung heroes and speak to those who conduct the stadium tours, which depart four times every hour — a tour which Douglas Anderson went on just a few months ago. What can they divulge, and do they believe they have the best job in the world other than actually playing for their beloved team? Before leaving Salford, there will be time to speak to some celebrity fans who hold Old Trafford close to their hearts, ranging from The Stone Roses and Primal Scream bassist Mani to broadcaster and diehard fan Eamonn Holmes.

It's now time to move east and visit the ground of Manchester City. Here are a team who now play their home games at a converted athletics stadium, originally designed for the 2002 Commonwealth Games. What changes had to be made to accommodate football and how does their new home compare to its predecessor, Maine Road?

In the post-war years, Manchester City took the unusual development strategy of replacing most of Maine Road's terracing with seats, giving them more seating than any other club ground in the country. It would take years for the others to catch up. Some of its design developments proved less popular and these will be examined. For example, the club replaced the roof of the main stand in 1982, and to many it was a costly and ugly mistake. The huge white canopy composed of 16 barrel-vaulted sections of glass-reinforced plastic panels, joined together to resemble a huge piece of corrugated iron, which did not fit in with the visual aesthetic fans would have hoped for their stadium. Who was to blame for this? The architects who designed it or the club officials who commissioned it?

We will speak to those who have worked at both, but not just in a footballing capacity. Both Liam and Noel Gallagher spent countless afternoons at Maine Road in their youth and ended up playing there in 1996 with Oasis. Some years later, in 2005, they would play City's new stadium, Eastlands. What are their memories and experiences? We will also speak to their friend and fellow City fanatic, Ricky Hatton, who has boxed at the new stadium. What did it mean to him and how does it compare to Las Vegas?

After Manchester, we take the short trip along the M62 to the city of Liverpool. Here we find two footballing greats only separated by Stanley Park. In the case of Liverpool FC, we find a club where the political and psychological aspects of football stadiums are intrinsically linked. In the history of stadium disasters, Liverpool have been at the centre of two of the worst – Heysel and Hillsborough. What affect does this continue to have on the club and what ramifications has it had on Anfield itself? For one, it has meant that the most famous terrace in British football, the Kop, is now all-seated. What made this terrace so revered and singled out from others? We will speak to those who once stood there and those who now sit there to find out. We will also speak to those who played in front of it and ask how it made them feel. We will discover just how much of a positive influence it had on the home players by interviewing such greats as Ian Rush and Kenny Dalglish. We will also interview opposition players to decipher just how much of a psychological-intimidation factor the terrace could summon and how that would manifest in the opposing team's performance.

It is also a terrace with a strange nautical history. When the Kop was extended and covered in 1928, the Kemlyn Road corner of the terrace saw a new landmark installed. It was a tall, white flagpole, which had been the top mast of *The Great Eastern* – one of the first iron ships in the world, whose maiden voyage was in 1860 but, by 1888, lay broken up in the Mersey docks. When the Kop was completed, the surviving top mast was floated across the Mersey and hauled up to Anfield by a team of horses.

The ground, like others in industrial cities, has been dogged with architectural problems due to the proximity of houses. Although the green light has been given to redevelop the stadium, we will see first-hand just how close these houses remained and chart the problems they have caused. For example, the Kemlyn Road stand's roof had to be angled in such a way that it would not cut out what little light the houses behind enjoyed. The result was an expensive stand that didn't cater for as many spectators as the club would have wished. Visually though, it was quite remarkable. From the top of the back wall, the roof leant forward at an angle of 45 degrees, leading to it looking as if it was in precarious danger of falling on to the pitch.

Back across Stanley Park, which was the site of Everton's first pitch when still playing under the name, St Domingo's FC, we find history still in abundance at Goodison Park, the first major football stadium in England and one with a multitude of fascinating facts. In 1913, the ground became the first to be visited by a ruling monarch, when George V and Queen Mary came to inspect local schoolchildren there. Soon after the First World War, US baseball teams Chicago White Sox and New York Giants played an exhibition match at the ground, with one player managing to hit a ball right over the main stand. In 1938 after the opening of the new Gwladys Street Stand, Goodison became the only ground in Britain to have four double-decker stands. The club even dealt with the problem of housing close to the ground in a swift and decisive way. In preparation for the 1966 World Cup, the club bought and demolished some terraced houses behind the Park End in order to build a new entrance.

More than at any other ground in Britain, here can be found the greatest examples of Archibald Leitch's architecture and design still in use. Should this be preserved or should Everton move to a modern, purpose-built stadium? We will talk to fans and club officials to gauge opinion on the matter and how much they still value their traditional stadium.

If football is a religion, then Everton are holier than most. Behind one corner of the ground sits a church, St Luke the Evangelist, where the Reverend is also official chaplain to Everton. We will interview him/her as both sexes have occupied the position and ask what exactly the role entails. Do they believe the stadium has replaced the church as the heart and focal point of the community or is the area just supremely lucky to have both? Is this the best example of football club and local community combining? What effect does this proximity have on parishioners and supporters alike? Are prayers said for the team from within the church?

We will again speak to former players and examine what effect the ground has had on them. Will it be similar to the experience of Alex Young, a key member of Everton's League and FA Cup-winning team in the Sixties? He once stated, "Goodison Park is a magical place. It's like when you go into certain houses where the great ghosts have been. There was something there that made the back of my neck tingle when I ran out on to the pitch for Everton, even when the place was empty."

There are more places for us to visit in the North West other than the big football cities. We will take a trip to Bolton, and a club who have seen a monumental volte-face in terms of spectator comfort and environs. Where now a Bolton Wanderers fan can marvel at the futuristic Macron stadium, the memory of the old Burnden Park is still vivid in many of their minds and was also immortalized in the LS Lowry painting, *Going To The Match*. This was a ground where, in its last few functioning seasons until demolition in 1999, had a brand-new supermarket replace the traditional terrace behind one of the goals. What effect did this have on the ground's atmosphere? Did supporters buy their groceries before taking in a match? Did they feel that their new stadium being named after a sportswear manufacturer (Reebok, until 2014) made it more impersonal, with too much emphasis placed on financial considerations? Will this dichotomy of financial gain against traditional civic and club identity be a continuing trend in years to come for other clubs?

Before leaving the North West there is still time to take in two more grounds. Firstly, we visit Ewood Park, the home of Blackburn Rovers. This is, in many ways, the archetypal northern ground, with tramlines, terraced houses and, until relatively recently, a mill all surrounding the ground. The turnstiles at the Kidder Street corner of the ground were used in a television commercial for Hovis, and we will visit the very spot where this was filmed. We will then make the trip to Wigan and examine the dual role of the DW Stadium, where football and rugby league are both played on a weekly basis. Can these sports really co-habit or do Wigan Athletic supporters believe their home should be for football only?

***

So there it is, the pitch for the greatest TV show never made minus the references section. When printed out, it reaches double figures page-wise, but it pays to be thorough, I suppose, when you're into an idea – and what has probably become very apparent is that I'm very much into football grounds.

Who knows if we will ever see such a show, but you just never know. As far as subject matter goes however, stadia and all that is wrapped up in them are a worthy cause for documentation and celebration. I'm sure I'm not the only one who believes so either.

17

AFTERWORDS AND LISTENING PLEASURES

As Kurt Vonnegut was inclined to say, "So it goes," but along with this, some final cogitations – which if also printed out wouldn't on this occasion require 11 pages of A4.

It's been the intention in this book to share stories that are of interest and entertaining whilst also adding in the visual accompaniment of a number of illustrations. But just as importantly, perhaps more importantly, hopefully, this book has shown that it's also possible to get out there, be creative and do something – whether or not you have an agent, celebrity chums or lots of disposable cash.

It might not make you rich or famous, but that doesn't mean you can't be an artist, even if it is self-proclaimed. Indeed, why wait for someone else to give you their approval?

As I've mentioned before, even if what you do isn't

to the taste of everybody, it must surely be better to receive criticism for doing something than criticism for doing nothing. That's the way I see it, anyway. It may even make you alluring to the opposite sex, but there's no guarantee.

By way of a parting gesture, I've compiled a list of 100 songs and 50 albums, some mentioned in the book, others not, but certainly all worth listening to. I could easily have put in multiple entries for certain artists but decided to go with as much variety as possible. I'm not claiming that listening to them will definitely improve your life but it would be very surprising if they didn't.

There are of course many musicians, writers, films and TV shows mentioned throughout this book that are also well worth investigating, if they have piqued your interest. They may even act as a jumping-off point to goodness knows where, such as a book containing broadcasting anecdotes, near-death situations, the minutiae of the album format, a secret passion for football grounds, forays into acting, and much else besides. But really, who would ever write such a book as that?

100 Songs

1. Serge Gainsbourg – Variations Sur Marilou
2. King Biscuit Time – Tears Dry
3. Bob Lind – A Nameless Request
4. Patti Drew – Beggar For The Blues
5. Nick Garrie – The Wanderer
6. Adam Green and Binki Shapiro – Pity Love
7. Bill Callahan – Javelin Unlanding
8. The Rift Valley Brothers – Mu Africa
9. Jeffrey Lewis – Time Trades

10. Peter Sellers and The Hollies – After The Fox
11. Francoise Hardy – Fleur De Lune
12. The Pictish Trail – I Don't Know Where To Begin
13. Lee Hazlewood – In Our Time
14. Mr Lif – Murz iz my Manager
15. Nick Drake – Time Has Told Me
16. Stephen Malkmus & The Jicks – Animal Midnight
17. Scott Walker – Time Operator
18. Houndstooth – Canary Island
19. Kraftwerk – Expo 2000 (Kling Klang Mix 2002)
20. Darker My Love – Backseat
21. Evan Dando – Ba De Da
22. Belle and Sebastian – Desperation Made A Fool Of Me
23. Tappa Zukie – Way Over (In Dub)
24. Townes Van Zandt – Come Tomorrow
25. Boards Of Canada – Zoetrope
26. Gene Clark – Lady Of The North
27. Camera Obscura – Razzle Dazzle Rose
28. Jacques Brel – Les F
29. John Barry – Monkey Feathers
30. The Fall – Edinburgh Man
31. The Middle East – As I Go To See Janey
32. Cat's Eyes – The Duke Of Burgundy
33. Markley – Truck Stop
34. The Warm Digits – A Warm Front, Coming From The North
35. Captain Beefheart & The Magic Band – Diddy Wah Diddy
36. Eels – From Which I Came, A Magic World
37. Alan Price – Sell Sell
38. Nick Harrison – Budgie
39. Brand Nubian – Meaning Of The 5%
40. The Advisory Circle – Wildspot

41. Shin Yung Hyun & The Men feat Jang Hyun – Twilight
42. Felt – All The People I Like Are Those That Are Dead
43. Lalo Schifrin – Magnum Force Theme
44. John & Beverley Martyn – Auntie Aviator
45. The Brian Jonestown Massacre – Got My Eye On You
46. Television – Glory
47. Allah-Las – Don't You Forget About It
48. Detroit City Limits – 98 Cents Plus Tax
49. Elliott Smith – Color Bars
50. Shack – As Long As I've Got You
51. The Rolling Stones – Jigsaw Puzzle
52. Fred Neil – The Water is Wide
53. The Beta Band – Alleged
54. Kurt Vile – He's Alright
55. The Kinks – Mr Churchill Says
56. Arab Strap – Love Detective
57. The Allman Brothers Band – Come and Go Blues
58. Broadcast – Lunch Hour Pops
59. The Beach Boys – All I Wanna Do
60. The Amazing – Gentle Stream
61. Chuck Berry – Let's Do Our Thing Together
62. The Smiths – You Just Haven't Earned It Yet, Baby
63. Glen Campbell – Guess I'm Dumb
64. Kenny Graham – Soho At Dawn
65. Hoyt Axton – California Women
66. Eagleowl – Not Over
67. Howlin' Wolf – Spoonful
68. Mandy More – If Not By Fire
69. Flamin' Groovies – Yesterday's Numbers
70. Jacqueline Taieb – Le coeur au bout des doigts
71. BMX Bandits – Fucked Up This Time
72. Mazhar Ve Fuat – Adimiz miskindir bizim

73. The Upsetters – A Taste Of The Killings
74. Pete Wiggs – We've Got The Moves
75. Veronica Falls – If You Still Want Me
76. Burning Spear – Slavery Days
77. Jean Paul "El Troglodita" – Everything Is Gonna Change
78. Real Estate – Primitive
79. Mogwai – Hunted By A Freak
80. Pye Corner Audio – Electronic Rhythm Number Two
81. Cate Le Bon – He's Leaving
82. The Proper Ornaments – You Shouldn't Have Gone
83. Air – Heaven's Light
84. Player Piano – Into The Dark
85. Mark Suozzo – Longing Suite: The Shortest Weekend/After Alice (So Sweet, So Sad)
86. The Phoenix Foundation – Gandalf
87. King Creosote – Klutz
88. The Phantom Band – Throwing Bones
89. The KLF – Pulling Out Of Ricardo And The Dusk Is Falling Fast
90. Here We Go Magic – Over The Ocean
91. Kid Congo & The Pink Monkey Birds – Goldin Browne
92. The Growlers – Love Test
93. Allo Darlin' – The Letter
94. Gulp – Game Love
95. Euros Childs – That's Better
96. Betty Wright – Sweet Lovin' Daddy
97. The See See – Fix Me Up
98. Bob Marley & The Wailers – Coming In From The Cold
99. Nick Cave and The Bad Seeds – When I First Came To Town
100. James Yorkston – A Short Blues

50 Albums

1. Bob Lind – *Photographs Of Feeling*
2. Darker My Love – *Alive As You Are*
3. The Beta Band – *Live at Shepherds Bush Empire*
4. Nick Garrie – *The Nightmare Of J.B. Stanislas*
5. Shack – *Waterpistol*
6. West Coast Pop Art Experimental Band – *Part 1*
7. Beck – *Sea Change*
8. The Rolling Stones – *Get Yer Ya-Ya's Out*
9. Billie Holiday – *Live At Storyville*
10. Houndstooth – *Ride Out The Dark*
11. Camera Obscura – *Let's Get Out Of This Country*
12. Jeffrey Lewis & The Junkyard – *'Em Are I*
13. The Beach Boys – *Sunflower*
14. Adam Green & Binki Shapiro – *Adam Green & Binki Shapiro*
15. Chuck Berry – *San Francisco Dues*
16. The Middle East – *I Want That You Are Always Happy*
17. Fred Neil – *Bleecker & MacDougal*
18. The Stone Roses – *The Stone Roses*
19. Gene Clark – *No Other*
20. Muddy Waters – *Hard Again*
21. Nick Drake – *Five Leaves Left*
22. Quilt – *Held In Splendor*
23. Flamin' Groovies – *Teenage Head*
24. Belle and Sebastian – *Tigermilk*
25. Captain Beefheart & His Magic Band – *Safe As Milk*
26. Howlin' Wolf – *The Howlin' Wolf' Album*
27. The Byrds – *The Notorious Byrd Brothers*
28. The Phoenix Foundation – *Buffalo*
29. Chet Baker – *Chet Baker Sings*
30. The Pictish Trail – *Secret Soundz Vol 2*

31. Real Estate – *Atlas*
32. Serge Gainsbourg – *Vu De L'Exterieur*
33. The War On Drugs – *Slave Ambient*
34. The Pastels – *Up For A Bit With The Pastels*
35. Scott Walker – *Scott 4*
36. The Growlers – *Chinese Fountain*
37. Big Star – *#1 Record*
38. The Smiths – *Strangeways, Here We Come*
39. The Beatles – *The Beatles*
40. Deerhunter – *Halcyon Digest*
41. Lou Reed – *Transformer*
42. Lalo Schifrin – *Black Widow*
43. Townes Van Zandt – *Delta Momma Blues*
44. James Yorkston, Lomond Campbell, The Pictish Trail, Raghu Dixit, Slow Club, Suhail Yusuf Khan and King Creosote – *Experimental Batch Number 26*
45. The Upsetters – *Double Seven*
46. Boards Of Canada – *Music Has The Right To Children*
47. Miles Davis – *Seven Steps To Heaven*
48. Television – *Adventure*
49. The Proper Ornaments – *Wooden Head*
50. Here We Go Magic – *A Different Ship*

ACKNOWLEDGEMENTS

I would like to thank Rebecca Lloyd, Milo McLaughlin, Scott Walker, Vicki Taylor, Peter Latham, Miles Jupp, Robert Secular, Frankie Boyle, Stuart Murdoch, John Reynolds and Nigel Thompson for their help and encouragement in writing this book and for the artists mentioned within it who continue to inspire.

ILLUSTRATION CREDITS

Douglas a la Gainsbourg – by Rebecca Lloyd

Two Hours In London – by Vicki Taylor

The Director's Chair – by Vicki Taylor

After The Evans – by Vicki Taylor

James Brown – by Vicki Taylor

Record Shopping – by Peter Latham

Fighting Talk – by Vicki Taylor

The London Nobody Knows Now – by Vicki Taylor

Belle and Sebastian – by Vicki Taylor

Steven Spielberg – by Vicki Taylor

Cathedrals For the Masses – by Peter Latham

ALSO BY THE AUTHOR

What To Talk About When There's Nothing To Talk About

A short book that's designed to help those who struggle to have anything to talk about at social events such as dinner parties where conversation is imperative.

Thankfully, Douglas Anderson has donated his opinions and standpoints to help those in need to go forth and socialise. If you have ever wondered why some women still insist on walking around in shoes with the scuffed price sticker still on the sole, why the word 'football' should never be abbreviated to 'footy' or how it is almost impossible to be spontaneous in modern society then this is the book for you. If you haven't, it may well be time to do so.

The book also comes with the link to the free audio version of What To Talk About When There's Nothing To Talk About on SoundCloud, narrated by the author.

Buy it on Amazon Kindle

Visit the author's website: mrdouglasanderson.com

Made in the USA
Charleston, SC
23 May 2016